I0617143

You're Not Listening to... What I Have to Say

PRAISE FOR
You're Not Listening to... What I Have to Say

La Faye Baker has been a life-changing force for good in the lives of countless teen girls. Her vision and impact are evident in her work founding and leading the nonprofit organization, Diamond in the RAW, and this book offers us all a chance to benefit from her wealth of experience.

La Faye is an essential voice when it comes to the next generation — both as a mentor and advocate for young people, and as a guide and educator for those of us who wish to understand and connect with them. Having broken new ground as a stuntwoman, carving a niche in the entertainment industry without a mentor, she brings deep empathy to her work. I am thrilled that La Faye's work and insights are now available to teen girls everywhere. These memorable stories will help a new generation feel less alone as they navigate an unprecedented time of challenge and change.

Areva Martin
Civil Rights Attorney, CNN Legal Analyst, Best-Selling Author, Founder & CEO of Special Needs Network

I have known La Faye Baker for the better part of a decade. La Faye reached out to share her Diamond in the RAW organization and find out if I would volunteer, which I did. The first time I did, I spent several hours with La Faye's girls during summer camp, and I was thoroughly impressed with Diamond in the RAW; it was evident that this was La Faye's life's work. Helping, uplifting, moving, and advancing young girls into confidence and assurance is La Faye's gift and passion. She had a wide array of volunteers, professional women like me, whom she had shared her vision and brought into her world.

She is relentless; she does not stop or give up, so here I am a decade later, still supporting Diamond in the RAW. La Faye continues to pour her heart, money, time, and passion into uplifting young Black girls, who are one of the most endangered species in the United States, and trying to ensure that the behind-the-scenes entertainment world continues to be a viable option for the generation of wealth for Black girls. She makes sure they understand their potential, provides financial education, academic enrichment, and a reason to believe. La Faye Baker is one-of a kind and has made this world a better place.

Karen A. Clark
Inclusion Strategy & Business Dev. Manager, City National Bank

La Faye Baker is a change agent and has created a road map to success for young girls and women. She is an educator and mentor to many, ensuring that young girls and women are exposed to her vision, passion for life, servant spirit, and zest for the well-being of others.

Her powerful presence in the lives of young people, has been transformational, exposing them to her life profession - careers in the Stunt woman/man industry.

Education is power and changes lives. La Faye's student-centered approach has opened the door for young people to reimagine their destiny!

This book provides a lens into the lives of young girls motivated and inspired to be the best that they can be! An amazing and encouraging read!

Sherri Lee-Lewis
Vice-President, Human Resources, Santa Monica College

Ms. La Faye Baker has written a stellar book. She reflects the transition from youth to adulthood through stories of racial discrimination, foster care, youthful angst, and the broader focus on the systematic failure of social services. She uses personal experience, optimism, and intellect to benefit others. Ms. Baker has done a remarkable job of keeping the vitality of oral deliveries alive on the written page. Her generosity of time, spirit, and personal resources has brought power to disenfranchised girls. I highly recommend this book.

Dr. Verda Bradley, Ph. D, LCSW

You're Not Listening to... What I Have to Say is an essential guide to getting through the perspectives of living that transform us, especially during the confusing teen years. Thank you, La Faye Baker, for providing a pathway to help teens navigate life's challenges with solutions to level up.

Stasia Washington
Managing Director, Senior Wealth Manager, Lido

I have the deepest appreciation for La Faye Baker's exceptional commitment to assisting teen girls who have encountered life's formidable challenges through the efforts of Diamond In The RAW. Her dedication and tireless efforts have undoubtedly made a profound difference in the lives of countless individuals.

La Faye's unwavering support and compassion have served as a beacon of hope for young girls navigating through difficult circumstances. Through the platform provided by her organization, these girls have been given the opportunity to share their stories and inspire others through this transformative book project. Her vision has not only empowered them to overcome adversity but has also inspired them to strive for a brighter future filled with endless possibilities.

Moreover, La Faye's remarkable journey as a pioneer female stuntwoman serves as a testament to her courage, resilience, and unwavering determination. Her trailblazing achievements have shattered stereotypes and paved the way for countless women to pursue their dreams fearlessly.

It is truly remarkable to witness the transformative impact she has had on the lives of these young girls. La Faye's selflessness and empathy exemplify the true essence of philanthropy and serve as a testament to her extraordinary character.

As I reflect on the invaluable contributions she has made, I want her to know that her efforts have not gone unnoticed. She has touched the hearts of many and has undoubtedly left an indelible mark on our community.

On behalf of all those whose lives La Faye has touched, I thank her for her unwavering dedication, her boundless generosity, and her unwavering commitment to making the world a better place for all.

Darrell Brown
Founder & CEO of The Rewirement Project, Retired Senior Bank Executive

This book of experiences shared by our younger generation will help you to understand the world from their perspective as we journey through their lived experiences...an absolute must read for all.

Arna M. Fulcher
President & CEO of Alford Consulting Group, Nationally recognized Community and Economic Development Strategist, Motivational Speaker

You're Not Listening to... What I Have to Say takes you through life, love, and lessons learned from living with depression to finding ways to build hope, will, and purpose. I would like to thank the author, La Faye Baker, for sharing this powerful body of work — it is needed and necessary.

My sister committed suicide at the age of twenty-six. She had been treated for clinical depression for many years. The one thing she said over and over again was that "no one was listening." I have searched for answers as to why she did it, and one thing I am certain of is that she must have felt very alone. I have devoted more than twenty-five years of my professional career to understanding physical and behavioral health as a clinical transformation consultant, college professor, and psychotherapist.

As a licensed clinical social worker, having treated thousands of clients with depression, *You're Not Listening to... What I Have to Say* gives readers real, rare, and really important insight into living with depression and finding ways to build resilience. The raw and honest reflections from women living with depression let the reader know that they are not alone in their silent pain. The statistics and factual information paired with the unfiltered personal stories create solidarity among those suffering from depression in their deep desire to be seen, heard, and understood.

Louisa Eyler
Professor of Human Behavior & Licensed Clinical Social Worker

I have known La Faye Baker for many years and she truly has a heart to help women on their journey. She is an experienced professional and definitely has much wisdom to share. I think everyone who takes the opportunity to listen to what she has to say will be enlightened and encouraged. As a coach, helping women through their various seasons is my expertise, I understand the importance of why we need mentors that are willing to share their insight and wisdom. *You're Not Listening to... What I Have to Say* can provide such guidance.

Wendy Gladney
Coach, Consultant, Author, Speaker

Life can be challenging for young girls and women as they start their journey. La Faye Baker uses her words and experiences as roadmaps for self-discovery and introspection, helping young women on their unapologetic paths to greatness, strength, power, purpose, and most importantly, self-love and self-acceptance. This amazing book reminds young women that "They are enough!" It is evident that La Faye's words are authentic and grounded in her life experiences, making this book a well of truth and wisdom.

Her advice for living an amazing life will resonate not only with young women but also with young men due to its simplicity and applicability to the fast-paced life of the modern world. La Faye is truly a Wonder Woman who continues to inspire the next generation of phenomenal female leaders with her life, wisdom, and experiences.

This book is a winner, and La Faye is a true "s-heroe" for sharing her knowledge with young girls and women, who are the future humanitarians, entrepreneurs, and thought leaders of the world.

Dr. Levi Harrison
Orthopedic Surgeon, Author, Podcaster, Fitness Entrepreneur

You're Not Listening to...
What I Have to Say

Stories & Solutions Curated by

La Faye Baker

You're Not Listening to... What I Have to Say
©2024 Luv What U Do, LLC

All rights reserved.

Library of Congress Control Number: 2024918827
ISBN: 979-8-9861670-1-5 (paperback)
ISBN: 979-8-9861670-2-2 (hardback)

Published in Los Angeles, California
Printed in the United States of America

No part of this publication may be reproduced, distributed, or transmitted in any form or by any means, including photocopying, recording, or other electronic or mechanical methods, without the prior written permission of the publisher, except in the case of brief quotations embodied in critical reviews and certain other noncommercial uses permitted by copyright law. For permission requests, email Luv What U Do at iluvwhatido2@gmail.com

A portion of proceeds benefits the Diamond in the RAW nonprofit, a 501c3 organization | diamondintheraw.org

Illustrator: Danielle Westbrook
Cover & Interior Layout Designer: Emily Anne Evans

*In loving memory of
Tamara Bivens & Summer Medford,
our beloved and gifted Diamonds.*

Preface

As I penned down the words of this book, my heart went out to the countless individuals who battle depression in silence, unable to open up about their struggles. These are the brave souls who have endured profound and unbearable challenges — a silent killer that can haunt them for a lifetime in the absence of support from peers, family, or mentors. In just two words, I can describe it: the SILENT KILLER.

Through the stories and testimonies you'll find within these pages, you'll come to know how teenage girls and young adults like yourself have managed to triumph over their adversities. There's a perplexing issue that many teens face — a belief that no one will listen or truly understand the grappling problems & peer pressure encountered. As you immerse yourself in these narratives, you'll witness how these remarkable young women harnessed the power of their minds to navigate through their circumstances and emerged stronger and wiser.

This book offers insight into the indomitable spirit of resilience that can reshape even the most unforgettable hardships. My earnest hope is that it will reinvigorate you, shifting your mindset, fostering trust, and nurturing self-love for those who may be burdened by the feelings of depression or the weight of past experiences.

As the founder of Diamond in the RAW, a 501c3 nonprofit organization committed to supporting teenage girls, I have heard numerous stories and concerns from our teen girls and encouraged these teens to share their stories. The results are a compilation, rites of passage and survival techniques. My primary goal is to shed light on mental health and address the myriad of challenges our teenage girls face during their formative years of life.

Within, you'll find compelling stories from our teen girls who have overcome formidable problems. It is so important that we provide resolutions and help teenage girls eliminate suicidal antics, depression and adversities.

What You'll Discover...

As you embark on this captivating journey through the pages of this book, you'll be immersed in the inspiring stories of teenage girls who triumphed over countless challenges, facing scenarios that could have driven them to the brink of no return. Each narrative delves into the causes and effects of these daunting circumstances.

The title itself, *You're Not Listening*, addresses a critical issue, while the second part, *What I Have to Say*, unlocks a treasure trove of solutions and reveals how other resilient teens conquered their own struggles. Within these chapters, you'll find valuable insights, alongside compelling facts, research, and studies aimed at combating these pervasive problems.

Moreover, this book isn't just about passive reading. It encourages teens to explore and express their own feelings by journaling their situations and experiences. As they put pen to paper, they'll uncover ways on how to navigate and survive insurmountable challenges. The realization will dawn upon them that they are not alone in their struggles; others have faced similar situations and emerged stronger. (You can, too.)

When uncertainty looms, readers can find solace in the outcomes of their fellow teenage girls. Each story is infused with EMOTIONS OF COLOR, painting a vivid picture of their heartfelt experiences. This window into their world will empower you to reflect and seek solutions, paving the way for personal growth and progress.

Journaling serves as a guiding light, allowing you to learn from the traumatic situations these brave girls faced and how they overcame them. By drawing inspiration from their stories, you'll discover your own path to resilience and healing.

In the end, this book becomes a sanctuary for teenage girls — a place where they can find refuge and comfort, knowing they are not alone in their struggles. Here, they can reclaim their strength and find the safe space they deserve to flourish and thrive. So, buckle up for a transformative adventure that will leave you empowered and ready to face life's challenges with newfound courage and understanding.

You're Not Listening to...

What I Have to Say

Part 1:
Problems

In Part 1 you will read firsthand stories of girls in their teens who have faced multiple challenges and unforeseen circumstances. In these heartfelt stories, they share deeply and honestly what they have experienced.

Each story is represented by a specific color, corresponding to the solution and resolution presented in "Part 2: Solutions." When you relate to a story, you can journal about your current circumstances. Just flip the book over to discover a way forward.

Stories

Systematically Denied

La Faye Baker

At the tender age of twelve, I came face-to-face with the harsh realities of racism. Growing up in a predominantly Black community, with an educator mother and a real estate-savvy father, one might assume life would be smooth sailing. But for me, it was far from easy. From an early age, I displayed advanced development, crawling at four months and walking at six. My inquisitive nature led me to observe and learn from everyone around me, even potty training myself. I felt invincible, believing I could accomplish anything. I was an adventurer in my own right. However, the bitter truth of racism and envy shattered my self-confidence.

At that young age of twelve, I participated in the National Hula Hoop Championship at Universal Studios representing California. I was the first Black finalist from Los Angeles, California. I had trained tirelessly and over 120 teens from Van Ness Park witnessed my unique and unusual tricks. Hula hooping was my passion, and I gave it my all, but on the day of the competition, the unfair judgment left me devastated and in a state of disbelief. As a young girl, I couldn't understand how a situation like this could occur. The judges stripped away my 1st place performance and I was given 3rd place.

The aftermath of that unfair judgment left a lasting impact on my life. It felt like life was unjust, and sometimes, titles were bestowed upon less-deserving individuals. My spirit was dampened, and I slipped into a form of depression, unable to reach my full potential. The knowledge that true winners might never receive their rightful recognition gnawed at me.

It was a crushing blow, and my confidence took a severe hit. I had put my heart and soul into performing innovative tricks. Despite the setback, our hula-hoop troupe, under Ms. Beva Lawrence, our troupe went on to produce three National Hula Hoop Champions and four World Guinness World Book of Record holders. I became the first champion from the troupe, twirling fifty-eight hoops as a world record holder.

Our team's talent was unparalleled, and we brought awe-inspiring tricks to the stage. I can still picture myself in my silver ballet shoes and shimmering black, gray, and silver fringed outfit, determined to win.

In the face of that disappointment, my smile disappeared, replaced by deep-rooted pain. Despite being a 3rd place National Hula Hoop champion, my accomplishments felt diminished in the shadow of that humiliating experience. The support from the Van Ness Park boys and girls couldn't erase the hurt of being cheated in front of them.

The impact of that blatant racism affected me deeply, shaping my adult life in ways I would only comprehend through therapy. I lost the motivation to strive for greatness, instead seeking alternative paths to success. This lack of discipline hindered my growth as an athlete and a true champion.

Even today, I continue to grapple with racism and discrimination, but I am a fighter at heart. Some may label me aggressive, but I fight fiercely for my rightful victories. Though I carry the title of a third-place winner, I refuse to let it define me entirely. My journey is far from over, and I'll keep pushing forward, seeking victory on my terms.

I am motivated, determined & driven.

Seriously, You Are Humiliating Me

Amy Jones-Jelks

Hot streams of tears run down my face as I stare at the teacher. My answer is left blank. Confused, I look back at the paper until she is yelling at me, "Write something! You're wasting my time!" I write seven. "No! That's wrong! Are you kidding?" My teacher continues to look down at me. "I'm done because if you can't answer a simple problem like this, then maybe you should go back to kindergarten." As she walks away, I dry my tears and wait for my mom to pick me up. I was in fourth grade.

Later that night, my dad sees me struggling with my homework. "Come here," he said. I sit next to him on the living room couch. "How was school? You have something to tell me?" I try my best to hold back my tears and slightly stutter. I explain that I'm frustrated, and my teacher is always yelling at me. A boy in my class would pick on me, calling me "retarded" and "stupid." Everyone seemed to understand math but me. I begin to cry again. I didn't understand why God made me this way. Dad's reply was anticipated, "God made everyone different. You can do things other people can't do, and other people can do things you can't do."

He reassured me that I was smart and not to let anyone tell me otherwise. All I needed was more practice and another way to learn. Most importantly, I had to understand that being good at math does not determine whether I'm smart. After the discussion with my dad, he asked for a hug. He must have felt my body was still tense because he says, "Amy, it's okay to cry if you need to." Then with as much strength as one little nine-year-old could muster up, I took a deep breath, and with those words, my walls came tumbling down. I cried, I screamed, I clenched my dad's shoulders as he patted my back. After crying for about fifteen minutes, we had a long encouraging talk and a prayer before I went to bed. I made it through the fourth grade praying on hands and knees, but I finished.

The next year, the doctor diagnosed me with attention deficit disorder (ADD). This was hard for me because it seemed as though life was handing me yet another problem. The way it was described to me as a ten-year-old made me feel like there was something wrong with me. For a long time throughout my academic career, a mental disorder held me back from my true potential. After a while, I used it as a crutch as to why I was not good at math. However, deep inside, I believed otherwise. I've always had a little rebellious soldier in me. Half of me thought I was cursed with ADD and it affected my performance in math, but the other half knew that wasn't true. I knew this because when I placed all my focus on the subjects I love or got involved and engaged with, I would excel. So, I thought, why not apply the same thing towards math.

I will believe in myself at all times.

From Blissful to Bullied

Brookelynn Fenderson

When I look back at my childhood, I think of the countless blissful moments that I had: from going to a Beyoncé concert at the age of four to engrossing myself in the fantasy worlds written about in the novels that I read. I will forever cherish those memories; they are dear to me. But amidst the beautiful moments, I cannot forget the pain and sorrow I felt due to the endless bullying I faced. My first experience with bullying began in first grade. I cannot remember all the details, but somehow, a classmate yanked on one of my braids for no reason.

The following year, I started attending a new school, and I ended up embarrassing myself in front of everyone. That humiliating incident forever affected the way people viewed me. I was so ashamed that I did not want to return, but I did, and my reputation was tarnished. Not only was I labeled as the "quiet," "weird," and "nerdy" Black girl, but I also became known for that one incident. The looks of disgust people gave me still haunt my memory.

In third grade, influenced by teen makeover movies, I believed I could transform from an awkward nerd to a popular girl by joining the popular girls' clique. I tried to befriend them, thinking it would lead to acceptance, but they had different intentions. They targeted me, making me feel like a worthless outcast. It became so bad that one day, I cried hysterically when my mom picked me up from school. She got involved, and the principal had to step in to settle the situation. That same year, my grandfather passed away.

In fourth grade, I faced bullying in my softball team instead of at school. My teammates made sure I knew I wasn't part of their clique, even though we were on the same athletic team. Fifth grade was a welcomed break from bullying, and I made lots of friends, enjoying a wonderful school year. However, everything changed when I started middle school. I struggled to find true friends and felt like I didn't belong. My self-esteem, which had begun to recover, came crashing down again. I started believing all the negative things people said about me and wanted to change everything about myself, from my personality to my clothes. I held on to the idea, inspired by teen movies, that a magical makeover could make me "glow up," gaining popularity, beauty, and everything I thought I needed for self-acceptance and others' approval.

Stand out among the crowd & create your own clique.

Depression by Way of Friends Who Tear You Down

JaNarie Rhambo

When you depend on people to build you up, they also have the power to break you down. However, you don't need their validation to know your worth! My name is JaNarie Rhambo, and yes, my last name is pronounced like the movie *Rambo* — and I live up to that name! I am a 21-year-old rising college senior, athlete, actress, upcoming director, and creative screenwriter. I attend California State University of Los Angeles, majoring in Theatre with an emphasis in Design Production. Additionally, I am part of my school's track and field team, and I work at Kaiser Permanente as a security officer watching Psychiatric Patients in the emergency department. On the side, I shoot films, do photography, and work with Megan Sousa and her comedy improv team 'Cornbread Kitchen' as a social media assistant, videographer, assistant producer, and PA. I know, I know, you may be thinking, "How do you have time for all that?" The answer is that I know my limits, myself, and my capabilities.

I grew up being passed between my mom, grandma, and auntie. My father left when I was about three years old, which was hard on my mom. As a single mom, she sacrificed a lot for me during the time of their divorce. She sent me to live with my grandmother, who was an elementary school teacher, for a while until she became stable again. Thanks to her, I was always at the top of my class, aced all my tests, and had great studying habits. As a kid, my family did their best to teach me values, chores, patience, love, obedience, and responsibility.

Many people didn't expect me to "turn out" the way I did. They would say things like, "You know, a girl with daddy issues is never a good thing." In middle school, I started background acting, and I had so much personality until I began facing bullying at school. Looking back, I realize this was the start of my depression. The people who talked about me behind my back were the cool kids who kept me around to make themselves look good. They constantly made jokes about my weight, and when I expressed my feelings, they brushed it off as a joke. This continued throughout high school, and I felt like I had allowed it to happen to me. To make matters worse, casting directors and other actors at auditions would tell me that I was too fat to be on TV, and I heard hurtful comments like "You're too Black" and "You're crazy to think you'll ever make it" daily. I began to let defeat get the best of me, and it was a tough battle to fight.

Surround yourself with those who will let your light shine.

When Forever Doesn't Last

Loran Marcella

Learning to cope with grief at a young age is an incredibly challenging journey. How does one grapple with the reality that a dearly loved person will never be able to receive the affection you still have to offer?

Earlier this year, I experienced the loss of my stepmother to breast cancer. Her battle with the disease had spanned five years, taking her from stages of health to sickness and back to health. Just the previous December, I celebrated my 16th birthday, and she was in excellent shape – no more chemotherapy, no more radiation, no more doctor visits. She was on the path to healing. Little did I know that my 16th birthday would be the last time I'd see her in such good health.

I can't even begin to explain how she fell ill or what transpired, but the abrupt call came in, revealing that she had only a few months left to live. My world turned upside down, and my heart shattered. It's a perplexing situation to come to terms with the fact that a person who was once healthy could suddenly be in a hospital bed, facing the end. The situation remains a mystery to me; it doesn't make sense. She had often complained of headaches, unaware that a tumor was silently growing in her brain. Witnessing her daily decline was heart-wrenching. How does one shift from robust health, regular check-ups, to a terminal diagnosis? It's beyond comprehension.

The last words she spoke to me were, "Are you coming back? I love you." Our final moments together were profoundly special, as she held my hand, and it felt as if she was passing on the strength for me to find happiness. Witnessing her take her final breaths, watching her gradually lose her grip on life, was incredibly painful. I miss her deeply; she played an indispensable role in my life. Living without her has been the most formidable challenge I've ever faced.

As if that weren't enough, just a few months later, my grandfather passed away. He had been grappling with various infections stemming from his military service, leading to frequent hospitalizations. Despite knowing that his time was limited, his passing still caught us by surprise. I wasn't prepared to say goodbye to either my stepmother or him. I'm grateful that I had the opportunity to see him in the hospital and say my goodbyes, even if he couldn't respond. I could sense his love for me through his presence. Witnessing doctors and nurses tending to him, aware that he could no longer care for himself, was painful. It's disheartening to witness the transformation from someone who was self-sufficient just a month earlier to needing extensive medical support. His death seems as though it wasn't settling in. I am not sure if it is because I didn't get the chance to say goodbye, or if it happened so soon after my stepmom. My brain is still in shock. The pain is there but the belief is not. I don't know, but I do know that I loved him dearly and to think that I won't see him again is aching.

Grief is a challenging experience. How does one reprogram their mind, heart, and body to accept that someone who has always been there forever will no longer be present? The impact of these losses extends beyond just me, affecting my family and loved ones, which is even harder to watch them process. In addition, attending the funerals which only serve as a needle of a reminder over the day that they left. Thoughts about what could have been said or done linger, but I often bottle up my emotions, avoiding tears. The pain is a perpetual presence, and trying to understand the unexplainable in an ongoing struggle of mine.

Dealing with the loss of two close family members within such a short span of time, especially at a young age, is incredibly difficult. Their deaths are not fleeting sources of pain but lasting reminders in every aspect of my life. I may mask my pain well, but it cuts deeply. However, I'm learning to navigate this process one day at a time, honoring their memory, and following the path that they would wish for me to take.

Praying one day I'll be able to accept the word mortality.

I Felt Powerless

Paris Bravo

I am a thriving professional working actress, martial artist, and stunt kid. I currently live in Los Angeles and attend Public High School. I have lived an amazing life thus far. Acting has taken me places I never thought I would visit in my lifetime.

Learning stunt work has literally had my adrenaline run to the highest point and to be lit on fire was epic! I would like to tell you my story. I am not sharing this to make you feel sorry for me or treat me differently. I am sharing this story to help you and inspire you.

When I was six years old, I disclosed to my parents that my uncle from my father's side had been doing things to me that no one should do to a child. My uncle had been grooming me for three years before he started hurting me. I had the courage to come forward. Of course, my parents jumped into action. Immediately getting the authorities involved to arrest him and get counseling for me.

My uncle was convicted and sentenced to his crimes after 4 long years of fighting with the courts. This was a capital crime for what he did to a child under the age of twelve years old. My parents never gave up on me and this case. My parents and my attorneys believed me. We continued to challenge my uncle's team to fight for the justice I deserved.

...and this too shall pass.

19

The Fears that Live Within

Angel Boyd

Fears are always going to be there. The more you ignore them, the more they sit and fester. Like a scar, they may never go away. I often think about those times when I let something stay idle and never tried to overcome it. It's a missed learning opportunity. You don't learn, and therefore everything stays the exact same. Now, I don't want you to feel bad if you haven't accomplished all your goals and achieved great success. We've all been there. Trust me when I say I am a huge overthinker. I don't want to be, but I am.

Although I do find that when I face my fear, it's a big relief to me and my brain. For example, my passion is singing; I love it so much! Although it took me years to finally build the courage to sing in front of other people. I'll never forget the very first time I sang in front of an audience. It was optional; I wasn't forced to do so, but I pushed myself anyway. Long story short, I did end up embarrassing myself on stage, as all the other singers had been performing opera since they were young. Meanwhile, my singing was very soft, and I had never sung without a microphone or knew anything about projecting my voice across the room. I felt awful, and when I feel awful, I overthink everything. Eventually, I came to my senses and found something new to think about.

Along with that, I've had and still have many fears in my life. I don't bring them up often due to another fear of caring about what other people think. I cared so much to the point where it affected me. Being a people-pleaser is a lot of work; you get so wrapped up in everybody else that you forget about yourself. I remember specifically this one time someone called me a people pleaser, and it woke me up. I had not seen it in myself until it was pointed out.

I have other fears as well, like losing my family, money, friends, and things that I've worked for. Insecurities about my appearance. I know everybody struggles with this. For me, growing up, I was never fulfilled with how I looked. I was always picked on, and in my pre-teen mind, I thought something was wrong with me. I was skinny, tall, and had acne. The thing is, I never thought these were insecurities until people would point them out all the time! I hated what people told me. When they did so, I just wondered how people were so rude and mean.

Maybe it's because I'm such a caring, empathetic individual and would never think to do it to another. It still shocks me to hear things that come out of other people's mouths. I understand we all slip up sometimes, as any person can do. But there's a time where you need to draw the line. I am working every day to let go of this mentally; it took me a while, but all I took was that leap of faith with the willingness to change.

Learn to let go of fears & thoughts that control your mind.

Living With Schizophrenia

Anonymous

Many people believe that struggling through life equals becoming a better person. This idea is probably assumed because of big icons like Jay-Z and Oprah Winfrey, or other highly successful people who have overcome hardships. In reality, not everyone can, and does, overcome tough trials. Many times, people end up having mental breakdowns, hallucinations, trust issues, feelings, and beliefs that they are capable of doing anything and everything alone because the world is against them.

Depression/Schizophrenia — this is something that I've been living with from a very young age. Schizophrenia is a brain disorder that affects the way a person thinks, acts, and views life. Individuals with a first-degree relative have a 10% chance of developing this disorder. But schizophrenia is only influenced by genetics, not determined by; therefore, those who are predisposed genetically do not always end up developing the disease. But in my case, it was different.

My father and mother dated at early ages. Neither graduated

high school but were married and had their first kid before my mother was twenty years old. Throughout gang banging, dealing drugs, smoking drugs, and making fast money, my father had health problems and mental problems. Fast forward to today, he's diagnosed with schizophrenia. Every day he battles for improvement. My mother is a single parent of five children; two have attention deficit hyperactivity disorder (ADHD). The truth is, she's been a single parent for nineteen years, since birthing my older sister. The difference between finding out my mother and my father's health is that my father's sickness was caught early. Because my mom was always busy working and taking care of family business, no one noticed what was going on until it had gotten out of hand in 2010. She was obsessed with the belief that our landlords spied on our homes. She kept us in the house, believing that neighbors were the friends of our landlords, who also kept an eye on us.

Two years later, my mother believed that the Caucasian race was the enemy. She imagined that neighboring and random

Caucasian people followed her while driving, even if we weren't in the same state or city in which we lived. At sixteen years old, I sat in a red truck parked in my neighbor's backyard, smoking weed. It only took fifteen minutes to walk across the train tracks to the best drug dealer's house, then walk back to the truck, roll the blunt and light it. It took two minutes after inhalation for an unexplainable fear to approach me. I remember my brain playing tricks on me. I believed I was seeing the night becoming blacker and had feelings of dark spirits surrounding me. I did not fall asleep that night. Instead, I laid in bed with my room door closed and my head buried under the blanket, afraid. I was terrified to move, to breathe too loudly, to speak. These were the first signs of undifferentiated schizophrenia.

The different types of schizophrenia are paranoid schizophrenia, disorganized schizophrenia, catatonic schizophrenia, residual schizophrenia, and undifferentiated schizophrenia. These types of schizophrenia do affect a person's ability to be more overtly or less overtly psychotic. The signs of being more overtly psychotic are believing in things that have no basis in reality (delusions), disorganized speech, disorganized behaviors, and beliefs that have no basis.

The signs of being potentially less psychotic are lack of speech, inhabiting facial expressions, and lack of motivation. Hard drugs and depression aren't the only reasons why schizophrenia is diagnosed. Truly, no one symptom can pinpoint the diagnosis for schizophrenia, though environmental and biological factors are thought to be involved. Early parental loss or separation, and physical or sexual abuse are a couple of causes for environmentally-caused schizophrenia. Men tend to develop schizophrenia earlier than women — this can explain my father and mother. The average age of men developing schizophrenia is eighteen, and for women twenty-five.

I am a silent warrior.

The Chaos Inside

Avrelle Lyles

It all started when I was fourteen years old. I used to be the happiest little girl anybody could have come across. But as I got older, I became very angry due to the way people treated me. Even when I couldn't help myself, I would always try to help others and make things right. However, when I experienced bullying in class, I started to feel scared to even come to school. I didn't care much about what others thought of me because I valued my intelligence, but the physical attacks changed everything. I began to isolate myself from everyone.

One day, a girl named Raven kept bullying me, and I couldn't take it anymore. I ended up hitting her in the forehead with a stool out of frustration and anger. It was a breaking point for me, and I was expelled from the school and the entire district for being seen as a threat to society. After that incident, I didn't know how to stop fighting, and my behavior spiraled out of control. Concerned for my safety, my mom sent me to live with my dad.

In the new environment, attending a continuation school, I managed to improve my grades. A year later, I transferred to high school at Washington Prep. I felt nervous, surrounded by bigger people, fearing they would harm me at any moment. I tried to focus more on my studies during ninth grade, but during my tenth grade year, I fell back into fighting, and it became much worse. I didn't care anymore, and it seemed like I was always ready for a fight.

I lost my boyfriend to gun violence, which further fueled my anger and sense of danger. As I grew older, I felt like people were after me, and I believed I had to fight my way out of every situation. The loss of loved ones, including my uncle Ronnie to violence, left me depressed and even angrier. I felt an emptiness inside, and my heart always ached.

I constantly fought because I was at war with myself and didn't know how to face my struggles. Demons seemed to be chasing my soul, and I was lost, not knowing what to do with myself. The pain and anger consumed me, and I longed for a way out of this cycle of violence and pain.

Forgive yourself for aggressive behavior as you change old habits.

Against All Odds

Carrie Bernans

My mom was a teenage mom. To make matters harder, the lack of resources and money put us at a disadvantage, especially compared to the kids I went to school with. But it didn't stop me. I remember in the early years of elementary school, crying to my mom about buying me new clothes and pants that fit me like my classmates had. She gave me a response that may have seemed fitting for her as a parent, but to me, it was always the same story, "We don't have the money. Be happy with what you have, and God will bless you with more."

As a kid, it's hard to understand this, especially because other children seemed to be doing so well, and they had the latest and greatest clothes. It was honestly challenging.

I was constantly moving from school to school until we reached a point of settling down, and every school presented a different struggle. If it wasn't clothes, it was something else — like one time, I didn't have enough money to go on a school field trip, but thankfully, a teacher stepped up and paid.

The story of the lack of resources continued, but one thing remained true: I saw my mom working two jobs to keep a meal on the table and provide us with basic necessities. That motivated me. Although many times, wearing the same shoes throughout the school year or clothes from Goodwill or hand-me-downs from church bothered me, it taught me how to make the most of what I have.

Create your own journey & success shall follow.

Rescue Me

Chauntel Browden

I never forgave her.
I always blamed her.
I victimized myself, in hopes to change her.

I couldn't get my way, so I went about it differently.
I thought that leaving her here would make her see, or feel, what I was trying to say.
I was a coward. Manipulative.

Trying to evoke emotions from one person, not completely aware of how many others I would affect. It's ironic, so many people say we "adore the ones that ignore us, ignore the ones who adore us, hurt the ones that love us, and love the ones that hurt us," and every time someone says that, I think of a person.

I never thought it was talking about a state of mind, a state of being.

I adored depression.
The pity, the suicidal thoughts, the hope that someone, somewhere, could come and rescue me.
I adored the idea that I could be saved.
A damsel in distress.

I adored depression.
The one thing, a recurring theme, a spirit, a battle that faces millions my age.

I loved death.
I had been around it so much, talked about it so much, heard about it so much, yet it was the one thing people talked about and hadn't experienced.

Say what you will, good or bad, but no one has or has experienced it long enough to tell you all the pros and cons. It was a crush. A crutch.

I wanted to go on a date with death because my infatuation was so strong, so deep, that I didn't want to think about what it took to get there.

The pain of planning it out.
The precision of execution.
Do you know what's funny?
If I really wanted to die that day, I could have.
I would have.
But I didn't.

There was a reason for that.

April 21, 2013, I was convinced I was ready to die.
Today, I know I was dying to live.
I cannot simply think about "that day" without thinking about the effect it has had on current relationships with family, friends, and people around me.

Even my adjectives have shown how it has changed and influenced me.

"I am a living testimony. I am free." I cannot continue, and will not continue, to live my life with regrets or blame. So, I must forgive her, but also forgive them. Thank them.

So, I forgive you, my stepbrother, for taking your life in 2009. For believing that the only way to relieve your issues was to leave them here. But thank you for the realization that there are two sides to every family, but three sides to every story.

I forgive you, daddy, for deciding a month later, in April, to determine your end date, without an explanation. I forgive you for leaving a message, intentional or not, for everyone who knew you.

I forgive you for making me overanalyze your death, believing that finding you was a message for me and the world to see.

I forgive you for sparking that fire, lighting that tunnel, that piqued my curiosity that I will ultimately not want to ever admit to myself — until today. But thank you. For exposing to me the reality of death, the warning of what happens on that date. If not planned, it can go so wrong.

A blind date can end so wrong. But thank you for helping, it has enhanced my testament.

April 21, 2013, I overdosed on pills in an attempt to take my life. I was ready to die. But…I didn't die, I woke up. Feeling terrible as ever, but I did.

I survived. I survived.

There will always be a path to happiness.

Codependency & Abandonment

Chinwendu Nwankwo

I am a twenty-five-year-old African-Nigerian American woman. I was born in West LA but grew up in the Inland Empire Valley area of California. I graduated from California State University, San Bernardino, with a Kinesiology degree and a mind full of possible career interests.

For most of my life, I have constantly focused on receiving the "message" or "all-knowing response" from my loved ones around me. I focused on this because I had no knowledge of tapping into my own confidence and inner strength. It took a lot of growth through various situations to truly find out my "why" for life.

Despite always having the support, love, and feedback from family and friends, I have also suffered from codependency, abandonment, and acceptance issues in my life. Recently, within the last three to four years, I have identified that I am struggling with habits and behaviors that I have been accustomed to since the age of thirteen. These are habits and behaviors that I am now trying to apply different techniques and thought processes to because they no longer work.

Many of the habits that I identified were formed from certain situations and consisted of isolating myself from others while still seeking validation of my emotions. I would always make myself available for others, even when I needed to say "no," yet I never learned how to set boundaries. I found myself being overly nurturing in every relationship. A lot of these issues stem from the loss of my mother at a very young age and my father being deported back to his homeland.

Unfortunately, many of my relationships led me to primarily seek acceptance from certain peers and the opposite sex based on my appearance and well-being. For example, in middle school, I felt driven to bleach my skin to have a lighter complexion so I wouldn't get teased. It wasn't until I arrived at college that I truly began to embrace being a Black American and Nigerian American.

Even though my father was deported back to his home country, I still branched out and found friends and a relative who were Nigerian, which allowed me to identify with that ethnic background. I then realized that "the darker the berry, the sweeter the juice" was a true statement and I had to learn that my ancestors came from Kings and Queens with the same complexion as mine. I also learned that having this complexion meant I was royalty, which sparked more interest in understanding the significance of my skin color.

One day, time will heal a broken heart.

Losing Touch, Losing Trust

Chloe Howard

Having a parent in the military has been one of the biggest challenges of my life. There's always change, mostly because we move a lot. Once we finally get unpacked and figure life out in a place, it's time to pack it up and figure it out all over again somewhere new. This is especially hard on friendships.

Most people these days aren't fans of letter-writing or even staying connected over long distances. So, for me, it's been a cycle of 1) make a new friend, 2) it's time to leave, 3) the friendship dissolves. Over the years, I've tried to keep in touch with people, but it gets old fast when you're the only one trying. You would think in this day and age staying connected would be easy. But I've had to learn through hurt feelings that friendship requires two interested parties to make it work, not just one. It can be really disheartening because far too often I find myself being the only one interested in keeping a friendship going. So, this just makes it harder for me to open up or even trust people.

Naturally, I start to ask the question, "Why should I form relationships with people when they'll just leave you, or I'll just leave them one day?" or "Why do they even try to get close if they really aren't interested in being around for the long haul?" Then other lies start to creep in, and eventually, a person just stops caring.

Then, I have to make a decision to accept the reality I'm forced to live in — either with all its negatives, or I choose to shine a spotlight on all its positives.

Friends are a growing part of life.
You might lose some but gain others.

One Swipe Can Change Your Life: A Blind Date

Anonymous

Alone in a college dorm on a Saturday, I swiped right on every guy's photo I found attractive. My two friends asked if I wanted to go to the beach, yet my body insecurities wouldn't allow me. So, I laid on my bed and swiped. Sometimes I would just swipe right because I was bored and wanted a reason to go out. While on dates, I felt "wanted" which was a feeling I never felt prior. My mother and father were both absent. My grandmother raised me until she began to date a man who didn't like kids, so she disposed me. Which left me with scars of abandonment. My aunt then took me in. Consequently, it's easy to understand why I would yearn to feel wanted by someone, really, anyone.

Online dating was great! Men would pick me up and take me out on dates. I couldn't help but feel special. I went out on several dates, so many, I can't recall every date. If I wasn't out one night, then it was the next night. However, It was about two weeks prior to the release of "Black Panther" in early February, where I laid on my bed and swiped. It wasn't long before I got a message from a guy proposing we'd go out on a date. Of course, I agreed. The initial plan was that we'd go to Newport Beach and later get food. However, the plan quickly changed. He picked me up in front of my dormitory in a black SUV. He looked and dressed comfortably: a white tee, basketball shorts, and Gucci slides, he was dark-skinned with long dreads. Although his description sounds alarming, I didn't see it as such. In fact, I was quite thrilled he was a Black man from an urban city considering we grew up in similar area and that my university was in the heart of Orange County, inundated with conservative, non-accepting people. I walked up to the car; we introduced ourselves and headed for the beach.

While on the way to the beach, his phone rings. He looks over at me, "We have to stop by my aunt's house." I questioned him, however, there was no response. I didn't want to overwhelm myself with worry, besides there's nothing I can do at this point, I am already in the car, so I continue to sit in the passenger seat quietly. In the car he plays loud hood rap music and drives recklessly.

We arrive at a hotel approximately seven minutes away from my campus. He threatens me out of the car and tells me to follow him, so I did. We walk to suite #XXXX inside is a two-story suite with a living room, kitchen, dining room, and bedroom upstairs with another bedroom downstairs. There are three other people in the suite: two males and a blonde girl. "Keep walking," he aggressively says as he walks behind me. He opens the two sliding doors to the bedroom and tells me to go inside. After he follows me into the bedroom, he slides the door shut and asks for my phone. I resist, and he immediately begins to yell, forcing me to hand him my phone. After I give him my phone, he walks out the room and slides the two doors shut. I can't help but think, how do I escape? There are no windows, and the way out is through the sliding doors. My heart races as I imagine every possible scenario that could take place once he steps back into the room. He's gone for several minutes. The doors slide open, he walks in stumbling. He forces himself on me and I resist by pushing him off. He then slaps me and begins to strangle me. I couldn't breathe and lost energy. After he stopped strangling me, he pulled my pants down. He tries to force himself on me once again, so I tried kicking him off. He strangles me again and rapes me.

I screamed and cried. It was all I could do. After he stopped, he yanked me out of the bed, telling me to put my clothes back on. I'm shivering uncontrollably as I try to put on my pants. Once my pants were on, he grabs my forearm and drags me back to the car. He dropped me off at school and disposed of me after he got what he wanted. I was humiliated and numb after the whole ordeal.

I am forever evolving, growing & eliminating old wounds.

Cancer Interrupted My Life at Nine Years Old

Estrella Uz Carrillo

My name is Estrella Uz Carrillo. I'm a college student at California State University, Northridge, majoring in Kinesiology and minoring in Arts. I grew up in Mid-City Los Angeles, surrounded by scenic sights and outrageous traffic. Something many people don't know about me is that I had a life-changing event occur when I was younger. It all started on April 31st, 2010, when I was diagnosed with a germ cell tumor on my ovary. Immediately, I was admitted to the Children's Hospital to have surgery the following morning. Because of my young age, I had no idea what was happening or what to expect with my situation. Everything seemed to be happening so quickly that I never had the chance to process it. I remember opening my eyes slowly and seeing the blurry images of my parents running towards me.

There was this overwhelming feeling of relief and sadness in their eyes. I remember being in a lot of pain, unable to move. I had to learn how to walk again, all the while trying to keep my composure and push through the pain. Over time and little by little, I was going back to normal. I was eating and walking on my own, but I had to be careful. The tumor was so big that after surgery, I lost a lot of weight. Two weeks after the procedure, I had a doctor's appointment for a check-up.

It was during this visit that I learned that the tumor had cancerous cells, and I had to receive chemotherapy. I was frozen. Being a child, I was naive and didn't even know what cancer was exactly.

My only knowledge of it came from TV, showing people losing their hair and looking sickly. For my first therapy visit, I was there for a week, connected to machines, and becoming weaker and weaker as the days passed. I remember going home at the end of that week, exhausted and unable to swallow anything.

Standing in front of my bathroom mirror, unable to brush my hair because it was all falling out; I remember waking up every morning seeing my hair lie around my pillow and all over my bed. My experience with chemotherapy has broken me. I wasn't the happy and energetic girl that I was before. I was completely shattered. I had become what I never thought I would be. I felt ugly and I was afraid. I had become paranoid, and I didn't want to be seen, so I locked myself inside. I felt trapped. When I looked at myself, I saw a monster that people would be afraid of. I went to therapy, but even talking was hard. I had a hard time expressing myself, and I cried every time I spoke about my condition. Everything had built up inside, and I didn't know how to release it. My therapist had me write what I was feeling one day, and before I knew it, I had written a few pages. It was there that I began to write. With the help of a mentor and family friend, I began to explain my story, my experience, as it went by.

I am worthy of good health & being resilient.

Abandoned at a Young Age

Naliyah Richardson

Throughout my life, I have experienced family problems with my mother. At the age of three, I was abandoned by her and sent to live with my grandma. As I continue to grow into a young woman, I understand how blessed I truly am despite this distressing situation.

During my early childhood, family issues always made me question my self-worth. Despite being the second child, I was always treated as the outcast, with my mother showing constant favoritism towards my older brother.

For the longest time, I felt unloved because my brother always received attention, care, and priority over me. Instead, I was always sent off to live with other siblings whenever I did something wrong, while my brother stayed in my mom's care. Living with my grandma was a choice demanded by my mother.

At a young age, this living arrangement made me depressed. I never got to experience the feeling of knowing my mother had my best interest in mind. She always left me stranded and made it clear she didn't want to be involved with me.

To this day, I realize the animosity comes from her being divorced from my father. She took her feelings out on the innocent me. Throughout my adolescence, I started to realize the worth of living with my grandma. Being in her household allowed me to find myself as a young girl and start to understand that the situation I was in wasn't my fault. I began to recognize my new worth.

While I was in the care of a family that showed me tremendous love and attention, I began to truly love life. Being raised by my grandma was a bright light in my future. She made sure I was healthy, educated, and well-rounded, while my mom never pushed me towards greatness. My grandma always made sure I was comfortable and happy, despite the trauma my mom caused me, and I vowed not to let it crush my spirit.

Learn to love & never look back.

Demoted & Fired

Anonymous

After being a solid student and athlete throughout high school and college, I took everything I learned with me into the workforce: work hard, be a team player and a good teammate, make sacrifices, stay organized, follow rules and instructions, be professional, adaptable, a quick learner, and coachable. Produce, give your all, do your best, etc. I had the keys to being successful in any environment! However, I lacked experience.

The only way you can gain experience is if you put yourself out there and gain it, right? So, your first job may be a little rocky. You're learning. I was learning. And as time went on, it showed. I made a few small [honest] mistakes that I was "written up" for, and it was scary. Every time, I learned something new about my work and about myself, but after one too many "mistakes," I was demoted and devastated. They moved me to another department where my responsibility and pay were lessened. It didn't seem fair at the time. I started to doubt my decisions and myself. I became angry with my bosses and less motivated to go to work and continue progressing. I felt stuck and unappreciated until I was given THIS reminder...

Don't take it personal. Another door will open that you can count on.

She Rocked My World

Jada Payne

I was only three years old when it happened, and my life changed completely. It is the reason why I am the person I am today. Though I was very young and could not comprehend what happened, little by little, I pieced it together. I was attending Optimal Christian Academy in Compton, California. I was a bright and eager little girl, always ready for what was going to be thrown at me — in fact, I still am.

My kindergarten class was having a field trip soon, and I needed money to go. My mom was going to ask my dad if he could pay for the trip, to which he agreed, and informed her to pick up the cash at our family business, the barbershop. Before we went to collect the money, we had dinner, something I remember so very vividly. My mom and I ate stuffed bell peppers, my pepper a bit smaller than hers and a bright yellow, yellow like the sun or an egg yolk. My mom's pepper, a deep red, the red you see on a bag of plain Lay's potato chips.

Once we finished, we were on our way to the barbershop. Then we'd come back — a quick, simple trip. But that was not the plan the universe had in mind.

47

What I was yet to know is that this would be the night my life changed forever and would impact me in various ways throughout the rest of my life. There was a gravel walkway to the door of the shop, and a couple of my father's friends were hanging out there. I said hi and kept walking to the door. Inside the barbershop was my father, his client, another barber, and this woman. I had never seen or met this woman before.

As soon as we walked into the door, she jumped on my mother. She began to attack my mom, and in self-defense, my mom pulled out her gun. This lady would not stop attacking my mom. She fought with so much force it brought them outside. My mom shot 5 bullets, the first four warnings. She tried to grab the gun but failed. My mom shot another bullet that landed in the woman's hand and lodged in her elbow. I remember the sounds of the gun going off, the bullets that didn't hit her going into the ground, causing pebbles to fly at my legs while my dad held me. I don't remember much after that, except the ambulance coming and putting the woman on a stretcher. My mom was gone, and my aunt came to pick me up. I was too young to understand what happened, so I couldn't feel anything different.

My mom never came back, and I ended up staying with my dad. He took me to go live with my grandma, aunt, uncle, and cousins.

I wasn't able to see my mom or schoolmates. I wasn't even allowed to attend school. I stayed with my grandma for most of the day, doing things like shopping, cooking, and going to the library. I enjoyed my time but still missed my mom. I couldn't call her and speak to her. She was my main parent, and it felt like she had just been taken away from me. I never went back to school. I was not able to interact with my mom's side of the family at all.

My fourth birthday had passed, and I had a nice party at Shakey's. Everybody I knew came, but my mother. I watched the door, guest after guest. My mom never arrived. For six months, I was without my mother.

Keep your hopes & dreams alive.

Why, Oh Why, My Baby Sister?

Saira Whitfield

Her name was Sabrina Gabrielle Whitfield. She was a twin, born on November 2, 2013, and she passed away on November 20, 2014. Sabrina's life had barely started, and she was gone too soon, too fast. I dreamt of walking with her to school, taking her to class, hearing about problems with her friends, and being there to help her through it all. At the time, there were ten of us. We are a big family and having each other was really important to us. Of course, we had moments where we fought and got upset, but that comes with having siblings and a big family. Even through the fights and the talking about each other, we still would always be there for one another and, of course, love each other. We're stuck with one another.

On November 20, my mom woke us up to get ready for school. Knowing that school starts at 9:00 am, we always rushed to get out at around 8:55 am. As our dad was probably yelling at us, telling us, "GET OUT THE HOUSE!" The twins were asleep, and the door was ajar. I peeped through the door to see them sleeping, so peacefully. I wanted to kiss them and tell them, "I'll see you when I get back." I wanted to stay home that day, but of course, even if I were a little sick, I would've still been forced to go.

After school, I waited with my younger sisters for our mother to pick us up, but she didn't come. Instead, my grandpa came to the school. It was a little odd, but great to see him. We drove back home, and there were a couple of cop cars parked outside our apartment. My Papa stopped the car in front of the house. We got out, and I felt like I couldn't breathe, as if somebody grabbed my heart. As we entered the gate, two officers walked up to us. My sister passed away. Gone. She had managed to get stuck in our double stroller we had for the twins.

My little brother alerted my mom and thanked God the week before she learned CPR. My mom tried to revive her, but Sabrina was gone. In my mind, I kept thinking, no way. This was not happening. It was the worst day of my life. Everyone came over, family and church friends. I couldn't eat. I wanted to scream, I felt so lightheaded. I thought I had to be dreaming, but it was the harsh reality. I asked, "Lord, this can't be happening." "This is my fault." "Lord why?" "What can we gain from this?" "What did you possibly want us to gain?"

I will always love you no matter how near or far.

A Desire for More

Jasmine Johnson

I grew up with both parents, but I still felt poor. My father worked a 9-to-5, and my mom was a housewife. I didn't know anything about being a spoiled brat. The only thing I was spoiled with as a child was my mom's attention. When I was ten years old though, she had a daycare and would babysit children in our community. Then, it always felt like I was sharing my mom with total strangers. My dad was very old-school. He wanted my mom to stay home and take care of us while he worked. I watched him take care of everyone but himself.

As I grew up, I wanted to be a popular girl and an honor roll student. I never believed in myself though. Due to this lack of confidence and low self-esteem, I was always looking for praise from my parents, peers, and siblings. I especially started to notice I had low self-esteem when I saw other students in my class that looked different than me. They had name-brand clothes and shoes. I knew I couldn't afford any of that but I would ask my parents to buy me all those things. They always told me "You don't need it,"

"You didn't earn it" or simply, "You aren't getting it."

I also started to notice the girls in my class had long beautiful hair. I begged my mom to straighten my hair or get it braided like the girls I wanted to imitate. At that time my mom couldn't do hair, so I had to practice myself. The girls in my class and their families had money. They could go to the salon. They could get nice clothes. It dawned on me that I couldn't get anything I wanted. I would always say life isn't fair. I started to become jealous and rebellious.

I started to become mad at my parents because of the life they gave me and my siblings. I would tell my mom she should get a job so we could have more money. I would ask my dad, "Why are you always tired? Why are you always going to work but you're not making enough money to buy me the things I want?" My dad was a bus driver. He commuted from Moreno Valley to Orange County five days a week, with only two days off. He was always tired because of both work and the commute. My parents didn't go to college; they just had high school diplomas.

Growing up I was so money hungry, and wanted to be rich so bad, because of my peers. I told myself I didn't want to be anything like my parents because I wanted the lifestyle the other children were living. I didn't know though that their parents were never there and they were miserable. Their parents were buying them things to make up for lost time. My dad always had to work, but my mom was always available. She picked me up on time from school. She volunteered in my classes for field trips. She would take us to church choir rehearsal and to vacation Bible school. My mom always made sure we were busy.

I had issues growing up. I didn't want to be tall and skinny with short hair. I wanted long luxurious hair and to wear designer clothes every day. I wanted to be an honor roll student, but I was labeled a slow learner because I wanted to play in class. I couldn't catch up with the other students. I would spend several hours doing learning activities, but it just didn't interest me. I had testing anxiety at a young age and was stressed out because I knew the answers but would still pick the wrong one because I was always in doubt. I used to feel like I was never good enough.

Soon I realized I had to create the life I wanted myself. I stopped looking up to my parents because they didn't have the life I wanted. Their parents didn't teach them to further their education and pursue a career. All they knew was to get a job and take care of their family the best way they knew how. One day, I woke up and had to erase from my mind the fact we were living in poverty. Erase that I didn't believe I was beautiful. I had to erase the low self-esteem and just go for everything I wanted in life.

Believe in yourself & change the narrative.

Mommy, Mommy, Why You Leave Me?

Haymali Owens

My name is Haymali Sinise Elizabeth Owens. I'm thirteen years old and have two siblings. The oldest sibling Alexius Arin is twenty-three and our baby brother Cyncire David, is five. Our mother is the fabulous Jeanen Kelly Meriwether. My mom suffered severely from bipolar disorder and schizophrenia. Sadly, her condition is what led to using drugs, and ultimately caused my mother's tragic accident. Because of her condition she wasn't in my life, and it really took a toll on me. I had so much anger towards my mother that I never wanted to see her again.

There are no memorable conversations or memories with my mom that I can recall. But with that said, she never gave up. She did call me sometimes, but I didn't know how to pretend like everything was good between us and we were in a happy space. I didn't know how to express my feelings or tell my mother why I was so angry. So, I just didn't want to talk at all. I felt abandoned, and didn't want to see her in the state that she was in. When she would come to see me, it was only to get food and water. I basically blocked her out of my life without knowing the consequences.

My regret is not answering the calls or trying to check on my mother. The truth is that my mom calling to check in meant the world to me. So, I guess you can say that she made me feel wanted again. May 5th, 2019, would eventually lead to the worst day of my life. My mother was brought to the ICU and was in a coma for five hours. The next day at 7:00 am she was pronounced dead due to organ failure from an overdose. I had no clue what was going on. I was at home with my grandparents and auntie. My dad was at the hospital with a few other family members. They thought she was going to make it, and I would come visit later the next day. Unfortunately, things didn't turn out that way. My sister Alexius Arin called my dad at 7:05 am breaking down crying and told him the news that my mother just passed away. I didn't find out until I got home later that day. Auntie Thea picked me up from the bus stop and took me to go get something to eat. After that she took me straight home and said, "Everything will be okay, and I love you". That same day I had gotten into a fight and knew I would get in trouble because my grandparents do not tolerate that in their house. I told myself, "When you walk through that door just face the music."

I went into the kitchen and saw my sister. I was so excited I ran like nothing was holding me back and I hugged her so tight and gave her so many kisses. Before then I hadn't seen her in two months, and we weren't really on speaking terms. I felt like she abandoned me like my mother did. But I missed her so much, I wasn't even mad anymore. I asked her to come eat with me but before I could get a bite in, my dad called my name, "Sinise!" I ran to him, and my sister followed. "Come sit down baby," my dad said. So, I did, and my dad says, "You know we all love you?" I said, "Yes daddy," and these exact words came out of his mouth "Your mother passed away this morning."

My heart and stomach dropped. I felt like my heart was tearing in pieces. Screaming my heart out and crying my eyes out, I just could not believe that he could say something like that. I wanted to throw things, hit people and I wanted to make everyone feel what I felt. But the most unfortunate thing was that I was the last person to know that she died. That made me even more upset because I never got a chance to say goodbye. I was mad, sad and confused at the same time because yes, that is my mother, but she was also not someone that I had a close relationship with. I never got to tell her I love her, or that I missed her. I never got to tell her why I was so angry with her. I never got to tell her that I forgive her. We never got to build a new relationship.

Her memories provide me with wings &
now I am flying like an eagle with ease.

Through Thick & Thin

Anonymous

I am fourteen years old and a patient at the UCLA Mattel Children's Hospital. Shortly after my tenth birthday, I was diagnosed with onset systemic juvenile idiopathic arthritis (SJIA), which is an autoimmune disorder. I remember being in perfect health one day, and the next day I was hooked up to IVs and lying in a hospital bed surrounded by stuffed animals. At the time, I wasn't fully aware of what was going on, but I knew that it would take lots of effort to get better. I vividly remember my very first hospitalization.

I waited in the ER most of the night for an available patient room. I was very lethargic and had a high fever. The joint pain was so bad that I couldn't walk on my own. I had chills and didn't want to do anything but sleep. My mom was by my side the whole time, but I could tell she was more concerned than I was.

Once I was admitted, there were two blood draws a day to monitor my inflammation levels and organ functions. Eventually, I would need a blood transfusion. Initially, the doctors thought I had cancer because of the many swollen lymph nodes in my body, especially my neck. So, I had two lymph node biopsies along with a bone marrow biopsy during my three-week stay in the hospital.

We learned that SJIA is a diagnosis of exclusion, and because it has many similarities to cancer, we had to rule out cancer before starting treatments for SJIA.

My mom did some research and found a pediatric rheumatologist at UCLA, which was much closer to home than CHLA. At UCLA, Dr. Alice Hoffman did not miss a beat, as she was able to pick up exactly where we were with CHLA. She advised that CHLA do a thorough workup, which made it easy for her to jump in. Dr. Hoffman helped me understand my disorder a little bit better and found the appropriate medications. I struggled a lot in the first year of trying to figure out what caused me to have a fever, joint pain, lack of energy, face and body rashes, as well as trying to explain to my worrisome friends that I will be okay. Although the doctors, my family, and I still don't know the cause of my flare-ups, we figured out a way to manage them.

The years 2017 and 2018 were rough years, as I kept flaring, and we were having a hard time getting it under control. Did the medication stop working? Was I growing? Is it an infection? Or is it a secondary malignancy from being on immunosuppressants for so long? When the outpatient procedures were not as effective as we hoped, UCLA Pediatric Team was quick to respond and made sure the transition to hospitalization was as smooth as possible. I was admitted three times from September 2017 to January 2018, for extremely high inflammation levels, which could result in macrophage activation syndrome. I had to be hospitalized to make sure my organs didn't shut down. They gave me many medications and shots each day, along with daily blood draws at 6 a.m. I also had to have another surgical lymph node biopsy to rule out cancer again.

Every morning I would wake up trying to put a positive outlook on my day. I walked around the hospital with another patient. He had his feeding tubes attached, and I pulled my oxygen tank. I prayed that everything would be alright for all the patients as we passed by the doors.

I am grateful for life & will live it to the fullest.

Is Beauty Only Skin Deep?

Shelbie Wayne

I was born and raised in Inglewood, California. Growing up was challenging for me because I am a dark-skinned Black girl with 4C type hair. I never wanted to wear my natural hair because I knew other kids at school would make fun of me. I was always compared to my other friends who had lighter skin and loose curls. Naturally, that created deep insecurities within me that followed me all the way to high school.

Growing up in Los Angeles, where colorism is a prominent issue, I always found it hard to fit in. I tried to find ways to make myself feel more included with everyone else. I wore weaves to make myself look more approachable to the guys. I talked a certain way and hid a lot about myself to please the people I called my friends.

Being considered a "pretty girl" was a huge dream of mine because I thought that would get people to really like me. On top of my physical attributes, I didn't participate in a lot of activities that my other friends did. It was almost like I was living two different lives. While everyone was going to cheerleading practice or parties, I was at rehearsal for a musical or dance show. At the time, it wasn't the cool thing to do. I was always labeled the outsider and could not accept that title for a long time. I put so much pressure on myself to be someone I was never meant to be in the first place and ended up missing out on some really important aspects of myself while growing up.

Loving the beauty I possess.

Really Felt Like an Outcast

Jazzmin Bates

At the age of sixteen, my mother gave birth to me, Jazzmin Bates, on March 31, 1990. After giving birth, she went back to high school to graduate on time. She attended school, then worked, and came home every night to raise me as a single parent. At the age of twenty-one, my mother got married to my current stepfather. Around the time they got together, he also had a daughter from his previous relationship.

As the years went by, they conceived two children and gave birth to a daughter and son. There's a large age gap between my younger siblings and myself. I was raised in a blended home. I didn't have a 24/7 relationship with my father, as I would have loved to. There were times I felt like an outcast or a tag-along. Though my mother included me in everything and tried to shield and protect me from feeling any different, it was still hard for me to feel a sense of comfort. I always had that void that I longed to be filled. I would see certain moments my stepfather shared with his three biological children and slowly but surely began to feel anger, sadness, and incompleteness.

I love & accept myself unconditionally.

Misconceptions & Perceptions About My Skin Tone

Trinity Fuller

I didn't always think I was different growing up — even though I was the odd one out as a young Black girl in the South who always had a majority of white friends. There would be little comments about my hair, or my skin but nothing more, so I just never thought anything else about it. When you are a child, it doesn't cross your mind that these differences can affect the way you're treated. There is something so pure about being young and not noticing the differences that we all have. Sadly, like everybody else, my peers and I began to grow up and the differences we did not quite notice as children became more and more prominent. Now of course there are many external factors that affected me, but, specifically for this story, I'm going to discuss the way my differences affected my self-esteem.

The older I got, the more and more I isolated myself from girls my age. I can't blame myself; I mean we live in a society where being a darked-skinned woman is not at the top of the beauty standard. It's an unfortunate reality that I still find hard to accept because I don't understand how just because of who I am, I am seen as less than. This always made me feel insecure growing up, I thought of myself as someone who didn't deserve love or appreciation from others. I always connected my beauty to the way I should be treated, so thinking I wasn't pretty meant that people have the right to discard me and devalue me.

I didn't feel worthy as a young girl, mainly because I didn't have much representation with people that looked like me when I was a kid. Shows that I enjoyed as a child had a primarily white cast, so the characters I related to were on a personality level, not looks. When I was at that age, I never knew how much that would affect me as a teen.

Once entering my teen years, my insecurities grew as I entered more and more spaces. As a high schooler, I was a theater kid and learned a lot about the entertainment industry and people. During most productions, I was usually one of few Black kids in the program. With non-Black directors leading the charge, I felt like I was never good enough for them because I never looked the part. Every performance or rehearsal, I would heavily beat myself up because I knew I had to work ten times harder than everyone else, yet I still felt like I was awful at performing. There was nothing inherently wrong with me, but these biases I grew up with followed me into my tweenhood and I couldn't shake them off. For so many years I just wanted to look and be the same as every other girl in my program and every other girl in my school.

It constantly made me feel much worse about myself compared to other people. I began to isolate myself and put myself down any chance I got. I felt like I was worthless because I felt like I didn't matter when I was the odd one out. Looking at myself, I was embarrassed to have to perform on a stage or present in a class. It felt like I was dragging everyone down because of every little thing about me.

By my senior year, I reached a breaking point with my insecurity. I spent my days sulking in the sadness in which I lived. I constantly belittled myself and felt like all my other white peers deserved these places more. But the difference between when I was younger and this point was that everyone could sense my pain. It not only made me weak inside but allowed others to prey on my weakness. I allowed other people who didn't work nearly as much as me to take my place, because I felt too little for the task. Mentally I was really struggling with my self-confidence and now looking back I should have been very worried for myself. When you get into that headspace, your world only revolves around your insecurity.

Every day I grow & appreciate my beauty & worth.

Hidden Depression

Rocky Avalos

My name is Rocky Avalos. I'm a Latino, born in Santa Monica, and raised in Los Angeles. I come from a large family, all of whom have had interests in art, music, and film. I myself have attained a B.A. from UCLA in Art and have been pursuing a career in costume design for film. I've struggled with depression, anxiety, and OCD (intrusive thoughts and repetitive cleaning and actions) all my life.

Growing up, my mom worked all day, and my alcoholic father was either absent or disturbing our peace when he was around. My grandma and my aunt, who lived next door, essentially raised me. I grew up and still live with all five of my siblings. We've had times of being close and times of being distant, hurtful, and distrusting of each other.

In middle school and high school, I hit some of my all-time lows. I suffered from depression, social anxiety, and had many thoughts of suicide. In high school, I truly wanted to die. I no longer saw a point in living, and I was revolted by myself. It was around this time that I started experiencing OCD thoughts as well. I didn't know at the time, but one of my very best friends was suffering from the same things as me. A silent struggle we both shared was finding our sexual identity.

At the time, I thought the only two types of identities were straight or gay. Had I known that my friend suffered the same as me, my sense of isolation would have been lowered. I wouldn't have felt like a weirdo. I wish we had felt more secure about sharing our secrets with each other at that time. Knowing that things can get better and that I can find people in similar struggles as me would have been incredibly helpful to know.

It's all about me controlling my happiness.

My Current Circumstances

www.ingramcontent.com/pod-product-compliance
Lightning Source LLC
Chambersburg PA
CBHW051625120626
46551CB00014B/1934

What I Have to Say

You're Not Listening to...

Part 2:
Solutions

"Part 1: Problems" presents stories by our teen girls identifying challenges they have faced within society. Here, you will learn how they were able to find resolution. Each story from Part 1 has a corresponding solution, matched by color.

When times are rough, look through these stories to discover how they overcame their challenges. Write about how you will find resolution to the problem you are facing.

Understand that others have been through what you're going through. You are a **SURVIVOR**!

Solutions

Claiming Internal Victories

Solution – Systematically Denied

La Faye Baker

It's amazing how the adversities we face early on in life can deeply influence the decisions we make as adults. The emotional trauma I experienced in my early years had a profound impact on my decision-making process as an adult. Despite having high ambition, there were times when I felt inadequate to be a winner. However, after undergoing therapy and adopting new methods, I have managed to redirect my energy.

Now, let me tell you about the value I place on winning. It is no longer about the actual place I achieve or how others perceive my success. The true win lies within me — did I accomplish what I set out to do? Did I give it my absolute best effort? Did I complete my tasks, whether it was for the day or in the grand scheme of things? Am I determined to win by never giving up? These internal measures define my success and worth, making me realize that I am the same little girl who won 1st place in the hula hoop competition, even though they robbed me of the official win. The real victory is internal before it manifests externally. If I give my best in everything, I set out to achieve, I am the TRUE winner.

Writing this book, I initially focused on how many copies I wanted to sell, but then I reminded myself of the true win — finishing the book itself. Each day, I work out diligently to pursue my goals, and that alone is a victory. Currently, I am taking on other challenging tasks that may seem daunting, but I am confident in my ability to conquer them. I am a WINNER, and so are you.

No matter what life throws at us, we have the strength and resilience to rise above it all. We define our own successes, and as long as we give our best, we are winners in our own right. Let this book be a testament to the power within each of us — the power to overcome and triumph in the face of challenges. Embrace your worth, for you too are a WINNER.

RELATED RESOURCE
Diamond in the RAW
diamondintheraw.org

Amy Jones-Jelks

After many years of late homework, name-calling, bullying sessions, crying and prayers for God to change me, I somehow managed to climb up the academic ladder earning all A's and B's. Unfortunately, I failed math. This affected my self-esteem tremendously because I always held myself to high standards. I wanted to be perfect and not being good in math in my eyes was not helping me reach perfection. I know now that no one is perfectly normal in everything.

The first day of high school came around and we had to take a placement test. Of course, I scored low, but my teacher Mr. Bonnie changed the way I saw math. He didn't teach me to like math, but he taught me how to deal with it. We met for tutoring an hour before school, at lunch, after school and even before taking tests. I saw the improvement in my grades and knew it was because of his dedication towards helping me to help myself. My grades at the end of freshman year were all A's and one B. That B was in math! I applied the same method throughout high school — constantly working on doing even better and going further. I even made it a goal that I wrote down on an index card and taped it to my wall saying, "Get all A's one year in high school."

So, I am proud to say that I reached my goal and got straight A's in

my senior year. For the first time, I knew that I could do anything if I worked hard. I know I'm not perfect and that's okay as long as I do my best and give it my all. I now know that I am more than enough.

College was a different story. I applied to four universities and all of them rejected me except one. There went my self-esteem. Bam! My mother tried to convince me that the college that accepted me was where I was supposed to be. The college was Marymount California University, a small liberal arts school in Palos Verdes, California. They had come to my high school and offered several scholarships to a few students. I was one of the students who received almost a full ride.

Instead of being excited about going to college, I was terrified. I had decided to be a film major after my experience with Diamonds in the RAW. I saw there were several fields I could pursue after graduation. Fortunately, film majors do not require math classes. In all four years, I only took one math class as a general education requirement. But to my surprise, most of the classes were easy. I realized that DaVinci High School of Design had really prepared me for college. After graduation, it was bittersweet. I was relieved not to have to study, go to class, and do assignments. At the same

time, I knew what I wanted to pursue, but didn't know how to get there. That's one thing about school: they lay out all your classes and your schedule for seventeen years, so you know exactly what to expect. Then one day, BAM! You're done. I was really lost at first and had to figure things out. There was a road ahead of me, but I didn't know what was the first step.

I quit my job at Jamba Juice and decided I wanted to work on my YouTube channel.

It's been one year since I graduated from college. Everything I've learned has been by trial and error. All I know is being an adult is HARD! Today, I feel fulfilled with the decisions I'm making, but I know I have a long way to go. I am working towards being an Influencer and monetizing on all my social media platforms. Nevertheless, I feel excited about what is in store for me in the future. Dad was right, God hadn't made a mistake. I am uniquely and wonderfully made.

RELATED RESOURCE
Online 1-on-1 Tutoring Platform
tutor.com

Loving Me

Solution – From Blissful to Bullied

Brookelynn Fenderson

When I got to high school, the bullying ceased. I was in a new environment with people who had no idea who I was. It was a fresh start that I needed desperately. It took me a bit of time to figure out where I belonged, but I eventually did find my space. I became involved in activities that I was interested in and socialized with all kinds of people. I even became president of the Black Student Union at my school in my twelfth-grade year and my friends and I ran the club together.

During my years in high school, I still faced a myriad of challenges, but bullying was not one of them and I am incredibly grateful for it. In fact, I had promised myself that I was going to be homeschooled if I dealt with the same mistreatment because I simply couldn't take it anymore. I had already suffered enough.

When I realized that was not the case, I was relieved. It was like finally coming up for air after sinking underwater. I could finally breathe again. Then, I had an epiphany: I had to accept who I was and stop waiting for people to accept me. Even when I attempted to fit in and blend into a crowd, I failed miserably. I still ended

up being an outsider, wishing that people would validate me. Fortunately though, it led me to the conclusion that I was already valid. I was already worthy. My voice did matter and as long as I was comfortable with who I was, other people's opinions of me were irrelevant.

That's the mindset that I have now. I surround myself with people who accept who I am and no longer involve myself with people who don't. I embrace myself in every way, so the self-love will overshadow my insecurities. I observe every part of myself, both strengths and weaknesses, both failures and successes. I no longer apologize and shrink myself down for being who I am. I am Brookelynn: a nerdy, fashionable, bookish, creative, stunning, fun-loving, jovial, kind-hearted, open-minded, tenacious, fearless, versatile human being and I will not have it any other way.

RELATED RESOURCE
The LadyLike Foundation
theladylike.com

Seeking Mentorship

Solution – Depression by Way of Friends Who Tear You Down

JaNarie Rhambo

All the things my parents taught me, all the lessons I learned, the prayers I prayed, and the mistakes from which I learned I asked myself, "Am I just going to let a few people take something I love away from me?" I started to make myself believe I was ugly and useless, no matter how many times people tried to uplift me. I was a very sensitive person who cared about everyone else's opinion. I was the easygoing girl who put other people's needs before herself.

I just wanted people to like me. I lost sleep, stopped eating, and cried in my room every night, praying and hoping for a change.

After a few prayers, I ran into La Faye Baker, a stuntwoman who became my mentor and life coach. Her Diamond in the RAW Foundation program opened new ways of life for me in my career and personal life. A part of her program that I keep with me today, even three years after graduating from it, is practicing repeating a positive daily affirmation that reminds us we are Diamonds in the RAW; we stand for ourselves, our family, our REAL FRIENDS, and our community. As we reflect life, we also receive it. We learned to believe in ourselves and that our destiny is designed for greatness. Being a part of this program and practicing looking at ourselves in a positive light and loving our insecurities was therapy in a sense for me.

I came out stronger, healthier, and smarter. I no longer let others run over me, and I know how to be nice without being a pushover. My family was very supportive during the process. My mom always told me not to stress over friends, especially in middle and high school, as those friends don't pay the bills. So, I had a better focus. I emerged from the program with a better attitude and body positivity. I appreciated the way I looked and changed the things I didn't like instead of crying about them. I started acting again and improved in that field. While in the program, I learned so much about myself and my interests, and I gained a love for screenwriting and directing.

Ms. La Faye's program, practicing daily affirmations, prayer, and surrounding myself with people who want more for themselves and for me is what helped me. I have heard so many stories from others and shared my own. I truly believe it has made me a better person. I will begin to write scripts and share stories of those whose self-esteem has been shut down, for those who feel like they have no voice, and to show others that if I can get through the storm, they can, too.

RELATED RESOURCE
Big Brothers Big Sisters of Greater Los Angeles
bbbsla.org

Learning to Cope

Solution – When Forever Doesn't Last

Loran Marcella

Life is complex, and as you grow older, you learn to navigate the emotional challenges life presents. I manage my grief to the best of my ability. I have a strong support system at home, offering a safe space to express my emotions, even though it's often hard. Immediately after their deaths, my words flowed freely when describing my feelings. To the contrary, now I struggle to articulate the pain I feel. I believe I've entered a stage of acceptance and moving forward, but it's difficult because I don't want to imagine a life without them. I don't want to move forward without them. I want to talk about my feelings, but I'm at a loss for words. Nevertheless, as time has passed, coming to an understanding that I can not change the past has helped me to cope with the situation.

I lean on friends and family when I need to share my thoughts and emotions. When I have nothing to say, I immerse myself in music, sit in my thoughts, and sometimes shed tears as I let my emotions run their course. I never stop praying, as I find peace in my faith during times of confusion and difficulty. Life is a challenging

journey, and the path to healing is unique for everyone. I suggest seeking out people you love and trust for support, as having a support system is crucial when facing difficult situations. Secondly, find activities that bring you comfort, sometimes talking is not always the solution. Being alone and happy in your presence can be very healing. And lastly, it's important to give yourself time and not rush the healing process. You will get there, one day at a time, as healing takes its own course.

While I may not be fully healed, I am learning to manage my emotions and cope with loss in a healthier way. Healing is a journey that may take years, but it's your personal journey, so let it unfold at its own pace. Don't rush it, focus on your well-being, and trust that you will find your way. I believe in you!

RELATED RESOURCE
P.E.A.C.E. Wellness Collective
pwcla.com

Paris Bravo

When horrible things were happening to me, I felt powerless and ashamed. My parents enrolled me in martial arts. At first, I was shy, could barely speak, and did not trust anyone. I loved watching my siblings train in Taekwondo, and eventually, I began to train and exercise myself. The transformation was remarkable — I went from feeling powerless to powerful!

Taekwondo became my outlet and safe place. Even though we were kicking, screaming, and using weapons, I started to feel empowered. Each kick and "kya" made me feel stronger and in control. I knew that Taekwondo would help me feel safe, give me a voice, and build confidence to get through the life-changing experience I had endured. Kicking the bag or sparring in class gave me a sense of control over my body and helped me release the rage that had been building inside.

During my uncle's sentencing, I was able to give my victim impact statement, using my voice to express that what he did to me was wrong and that no child should go through such a traumatic experience. I also emphasized that I had to be strong, not just for myself, but for others, to prevent him from harming other children. After the Judge delivered a stern scolding, he was sentenced and taken straight to prison.

Becoming an actress has also been a source of healing for me. It allows me to be someone else, and in emotionally charged scenes, I draw from my own memories of fear and vulnerability to bring

authenticity to my performances. Acting has played a significant role in my survival and personal growth.

I want you to know that you are not alone in facing this kind of trauma. Sadly, these acts occur every day, often perpetrated by someone trusted, be it a family member or friend. I've chosen not to be a victim; instead, I choose to be a victor! I use the power within me to confront my nightmares and memories. My acting is a channel for this terror, helping me cope and heal.

Remember, your voice matters, and you have the strength to turn your situation into something great. After high school, I plan to attend UCLA and pursue a degree in Childhood Psychology to help children process what I have gone through. Acting and stunts will remain passions of mine, but when I'm not performing, I want to dedicate myself to helping others.

If you are experiencing something similar, please don't hesitate to tell someone. If sharing with a family member feels uncomfortable, reach out to the appropriate authorities or seek professional help. You deserve support and care; no one should have to go through this alone. Remember, you are loved and needed. Your voice is powerful, and you can make a difference in your own life and the lives of others.

RELATED RESOURCE
National Child Abuse Coalition
nationalchildabusecoalition.org

Angel Boyd

As I grew older, I realized that people picking on me was their way of venting out their insecurities, as they lacked confidence in themselves. It's mainly because the world around us has ingrained the belief that perfect people exist, especially for girls and women. Beauty standards impose unrealistic expectations of having flawless hair, skin, nails, body, attitude, face, money, family, complexion, clothes, and so on, just to fit into a certain category. Deep down, we all know this isn't realistic, but societal conditioning makes us believe otherwise. Even if someone appears perfect at first glance, we never truly know what they are going through.

The phrase "never judge a book by its cover" holds significant truth. Subconsciously, we all judge each other daily just by appearances. However, we have a choice in how we react to others and what we say. We also have control over where we invest our energy, as it's a potent force that others can feel more than we might think.

When I went on stage to sing for the first time, I was nervous, and my mom and friends shared the same anxiety. The fear inside me was so intense that I couldn't even hear the audience's applause. Looking back, I wish I had approached it with love instead of fear, which might have made it easier to overcome. Now, my best

friend and I love trying new things, even if it sometimes feels embarrassing. Our motto, "Nobody Cares," keeps us going. I firmly believe that nobody cares about you more than yourself. When you do something, it remains in your memory, but others may react momentarily and then move on with their lives. Worrying about what others think will never lead you anywhere fruitful. Every step you took in your past has led you to this very moment of reading my paper.

So, remember to embrace self-acceptance, love, and validation, knowing that societal expectations of perfection are unrealistic. Choose how you react to others and what you invest your energy in. Don't be held back by the fear of judgment or the need for approval. Focus on your own growth and recognize that your past experiences have brought you to where you are now. Trust in yourself and live life on your terms, not dictated by external opinions.

RELATED RESOURCE
HipLatina
hiplatina.com

Understanding the Options

Anonymous

There are so many solutions to get rid of, or at least minimize the chances of depression and schizophrenia. Two solutions that are common are medication and psychosocial interventions. I believe that medicine helps those who aren't able to live with a normal mindset on a daily basis until progress is proven. Psychosocial interventions are helpful because it includes support from doctors and specialists.

Ultimately, I believe support is helpful when dealing with a person or people who are affected by schizophrenia. Medication remains as the key element of treatment for people with schizophrenia. It decreases the intensity of psychotic symptoms, and it is thought to be particularly effective in treating positive symptoms of schizophrenia. I do not believe that all people diagnosed with schizophrenia should be subject to take medication drugs. Of course, not all types of schizophrenia are the same and they do not lead to the same mental damages, therefore there are many medications that are available to fit particular needs. My mother and father both take prescribed medication for their illness. I believe that many diagnosed with schizophrenia should take medication, because of how dangerous a person who carries it can be in certain situations.

Psychosocial interventions include social-skills training, behavior therapy, substance abuse treatment, and weight management.

Social-skills training teaches schizophrenics many ways to handle social situations appropriately. This has been found to help those diagnosed with schizophrenia resist drug abuse, and even improve relationships. Cognitive Behavior therapy (CBT) focuses on helping a person with their daily patterns and abilities to interact with others and function correctly. 50% of individuals with schizophrenia suffer from a form of substance abuse. Substance abuse treatment provides medical and psychological interventions about substance abuse and how it should be encountered within 100% of individual recovery sessions. Weight management deals with the aftereffects of medication. Weight loss and weight gain are both common when taking prescribed pills.

And lastly, support comes in many forms. Simple acts like assisting a person when calling a crisis hotline, referring one to enroll in a hospital, communicating with that person — showing him/her affected with schizophrenia that you are by their side to be a support system, these are the many different ways to support a person. Preventing schizophrenia is difficult, and in my opinion, almost impossible. But I believe that we as people can lend a helping hand and support one another.

RELATED RESOURCE
National Alliance on Mental Illness
nami.org

Gaining Self-Control

Solution – The Chaos Inside

Av'relle Lyles

My life got really difficult and sometimes I just wanted to give up on myself. At that point my soul was gone and had to find a way to get it back. I didn't want to be that angry little girl anymore. My 12th grade year came around, and I had a lot of improvement to do. My education depended on it. So, I stepped my game up. Months went by where I didn't fight at all. I was all about school, sports, and video production with my teacher, Mr. McCane at Washington Prep. Video production made me so happy and I loved watching my work. A lot of teachers saw the good in me, but I still saw the bad in myself.

2018 came around and I lost a friend due to police brutality. AJ was my roll dawg. Always smiling and always happy. I heard the shots and ran as fast as I could, but by then he was already gone. I cried because there was nothing I could do. It ate me up so bad. I lost myself a lot, but I also had things I needed to prove to myself. So, I began to see a therapist at Washington Prep. I pushed myself every day until graduation and I finally graduated in the class of 2018. I was so proud of myself! I made it. I did it for everyone I lost, my family, my friends, and myself.

RELATED RESOURCE
National Association of People Against Bullying
napab.org

Developing Discipline

Solution – Against All Odds

Carrie Bernans

I think it is often easy to look at stories like mine and think, "Oh, poor child," "she moved around constantly, didn't have enough resources to do things that are provided to kids who may have more financial support," etc. But the truth, according to Bloomberg, is that "More than 1 in 10 American children spend more than half their childhood in poverty — that's a whopping nine million kids." So, I wasn't the only one. Most of these children are trapped in a cycle of deficiency, lacking education, mental support, basic necessities, and more. As young adults, they're unlikely to be in school or working, and sadly, if they have children, they often follow a similar path. However, a small percentage, of which I am thankful to be one, managed to escape their circumstances and become economically successful.

What I believe differentiates these children and myself, and what can help the children of the future born into poverty are three major things: behavior, mentorship, and education. Now, although these three things play a huge significance in growing out of poverty, I do acknowledge that some things are out of a kid's control, such as treatment from their parents, living situations, having a job at a young age, etc. But let's break down these three for now: behavior, mentorship, and education.

Behavior is everything. Mindset is everything. Although I knew I

was poor and lacked resources as a kid, I didn't often say it aloud. I remember daydreaming for better days, writing my visions down for the future. I kept telling everyone about my big dreams of being the president of the United States or CEO of an international corporation or a big Hollywood actress. Although some may not have fully believed me or thought I was just a big dreamer, it started growing my confidence, which ultimately affected my behavior and how I processed certain things and looked at situations. Instead of being upset about things, I started imagining that bigger things were to come, and one day, what I have overcome will be a testimony to many kids growing up like I did. Some of the quotes I learned and remembered were "Tough times never last, but tough people do." – Robert Schuller | "When everything seems to be going against you, remember that the airplane takes off against the wind, not with it." – Henry Ford | "It doesn't matter how slow you go, as long as you don't stop." – Confucius | And ultimately, I leave you with this...Write your vision down. Make a plan. Just like Habakkuk 2:2 says in the Bible. Write it down. Make actionable steps. Change your thinking behavior. Remember you are a light even in dark places, and this too shall pass...and only make you stronger.

Mentorship is everything. I'm so grateful for my first mentors who were my teachers. Even my mom, who, although struggling

in her own ways, managed two growing children and pushed me substantially to become the person I am today. Although I didn't make it known at school that we were barely making it sometimes, or I didn't have enough money for something, teachers would randomly say positive words to me, pull me aside, ask me if I was okay, or suggest that I do a science project or something. At the time, I didn't think about how big of an impact that really was until my almost early teenage years. Without them playing the role of "silent mentors," I wouldn't have gone to half of the summer camps they suggested, tried out for the track team, joined the honors club, etc., which all had a huge impact on who I am today. And as I continued to grow, I had an opportunity to get mentors through the Big Brothers, Big Sisters Club, YMCA programs, Youth About Business, and more. Through those mentorships, it stretched me, grew me, and introduced me to a whole other world I never knew about. I learned about stocks and 10Ks...even wrote my first annual report through a simulation business camp through Youth About Business. I won a shopping spree which was a huge surprise and very much needed, and by the YMCA and Target, which ended up with me doing my own giveback with kids every Christmas through my nonprofit CBSeed, and even more. I highly suggest everyone get a mentor at every stage of life, no matter how young or old you are.

Education is everything. I am not one to say that every kid needs to go to college or that every kid doesn't. But gaining skills is vital. And depending on your desired career path, education is key. Education is a big make-or-break factor in how kids break out of poverty and become successful. The educational gap between rich kids and poor kids increases daily because, first off, kids that are poor are already born into segregated schooling due to property taxes funding schools.

Schools in poorer neighborhoods, which have lower property taxes due to the lower home costs, are significantly different from schools in richer neighborhoods, which have significantly higher property taxes. So, with a lack of resources in poorer schools, underfunded teachers, and everything else, kids born into poor communities have to work harder, take extra programs, study harder, and catch up on lots of lost learning. I knew this early on when going to school because I attended schools in poor communities and rich ones — not because my mom was anywhere near rich when I was younger, but because she fought extremely hard to get us into better school districts and pushed us to read, write, and work every day to be smarter.

My mom is the reason why I worked my butt off in school and in

sports. First off, I didn't want to ever be poor or near the poverty lines again, and secondly, I wanted to be living proof that kids anywhere can be anything if you work hard enough to get there. Was it easy? No. Was it worth it? 1000000% YES. As Nelson Mandela said, "Education is the most powerful weapon which you can use to change the world." So, if you have to take tutoring after school, take it. If you have a chance to do a science fair project, do it. If you are given the opportunity to stand up for someone, do it. Whatever you do, don't limit yourself.

KNOW THIS: We are limitless beyond our imaginations. We must not limit our growth or ourselves. We must dream big and challenge anything that tries to tell us otherwise. We can and will change the world. When negative thoughts come into your head, flip it and reverse it. No matter how great the circumstances you experience are, know that you can get through them with faith and perseverance. Faith without works is dead, babe. Take some action and go after it!

RELATED RESOURCE
EmpowHer Institute
empowher.org

Moving Forward

Solution – Rescue Me

Chauntel Browden

Looking back on my experience, I have learned a few things.
I learned that I do not need to please everyone.
I learned that I cannot please everyone.
I learned that I will not please everyone.
I learned that time, in itself, is a lesson that teaches us all.
I learned that pain is an inevitable gift that teaches someone to grow stronger.

I learned that I am a survivor.
I survived.
A friend of mine once told me that if you don't die when logically you should have, that's God telling you it's not your time yet. And I believe that.
I realized that pain is the worst thing to hold onto because it literally, physically, weighs you down.
It eats away at your heart, your mind, your body, and your soul.
For years, I was adoring depression and loving death.

Then I jumped into a marriage with depression, having an affair with death. But my scandal was exposed.

By the grace of God, I can proudly say I have ended it.
Hey, I've finalized it.
By writing this, I have signed my divorce papers with depression.

I have ended my abusive relationship with death.
I have cleared my time, changed my life.
As I close this chapter of my life and start on the next, my spirit can now soar free.
I am uniquely, entirely, solely me.
You know my name, but not my story. However, by the power invested in me, you now have a glimpse of my testimony.

RELATED RESOURCE
Amen Clinics
amenclinics.com

Exercising Patience

Solution – Codependency & Abandonment

Chinwendu Nwankwo

Fortunately, I am now on a steadier path towards understanding the true meaning of self-acceptance, self-love, and self-validation. I have learned to appreciate the challenging moments and take each day as it comes. Reminding myself that reactive behavior is a choice has helped me become more patient with myself.

I am grateful for knowing how to set healthy boundaries and prioritize my peace of mind. I understand that transforming my mindset is a lifelong process and cannot be mastered in just three to six months. I am still growing, and the journey to truly loving everything about myself continues.

RELATED RESOURCE
Therapy For Black Girls
therapyforblackgirls.com

Building Genuine Friendship

Solution – Losing Touch, Losing Trust

Chloe Howard

After eight moves in less than thirteen years, it has definitely shaped me. I am grateful for all of my memories and moments. I am glad to have a wonderful family who really loves and cares about me and makes traveling a worthwhile and fun part of what we do. All the scores of pictures and laughs collected from all the places we've been, and the friends who do call and visitors who come to us definitely keep me uplifted. All the opportunities galore to experience different cultures by taste touring and local exploring surely outweigh being stuck in one place.

Just learning to enjoy the time while I am in it without expectations for more has been the new lesson and practice for me. Homeschooling has definitely made it much easier too because I've been able to focus on my music, art, writing, and building my YouTube Channel, Kitty & Queen.

Some people are fortunate enough not to go through the cycle as often as we have. Yet, despite my personal hardships of being an Army kid, it is also very encouraging because it builds character and mental toughness. Additionally, I've been able to learn at a young age how to put time and energy into only genuine relationships that have time and energy for me.

RELATED RESOURCE
Operation We Are Here
operationwearehere.com

Acknowledging the Truth

Solution – One Swipe Can Change Your Life: A Blind Date

Anonymous

For months I battled and blamed myself for what happened. It wasn't until I went to counseling that I began to feel comfortable enough to open up about the rape. I finally felt a release. I realized I made the choice to get in the car, but I didn't choose to be raped. My virginity was unrightfully taken from me that night. Acknowledgement and acceptance are what helped me forgive myself. I first had to acknowledge what happened to me and no longer live in denial and feel embarrassed about being a victim. Most importantly I had to accept that it happened and that it is a chapter in my life that I was able to overcome. It took a year for me to fully face the trauma I endured and ever since, I've been happier.

Now I have the courage to educate people of the dangers of online dating and openly talk about my experiences encountering sexual assault. That one swipe right didn't just change my life, but turned me into a survivor.

RELATED RESOURCE
National Sexual Violence Resource Center
nsvrc.org

Staying Determined

Solution – Cancer Interrupted My Life at Nine Years Old

Estrella Uz Carrillo

By the end of summer, I was given the best news of my life: I was cancer free! I had spent so much time in the hospital. Having to wait and be patient. Endless nights unable to sleep from feeling sick. Unable to go anywhere and confined within the walls of the hospital. Unable to eat and feeling nauseous from seeing or smelling anything. Having my natural skin color change and looking very pale. And worst of all, losing all of my hair.

It took more than a year for me to fully recover, physically and mentally. I had to learn to express myself again, to feel comfortable in my own skin, to be myself. It required many therapy sessions and just going back to my regular routine. With the help of my family, friends and even writing, I became stronger. It's been about ten years now. I am healthy, strong and living my life as much as I can. I continue to be thankful for my life and the chance to come back. There are so many children in the hospital that don't get that second chance and have had it way worse. Some that continue to battle, and that reminds me to stay humble and be grateful to be standing where I am today. After going through so much, my battle is over, now my journey begins.

RELATED RESOURCE
Cancer Center for Children & Teens
choc.org/cancer

Letting Go

Solution – Abandoned at a Young Age

Naliyah Richardson

Looking back at life, I don't regret not having my mom in my life because I believe that if she had been around, I wouldn't be the outgoing, passionate, educated, independent, and wise young lady I am today. My grandma has been the one who raised me and molded me into the best version of myself. I don't regret my childhood at all!

RELATED RESOURCE
United Friends
unitedfriends.org

Focusing on the Positive

Solution – Demoted & Fired

Anonymous

"Remember why you're there!" I initially moved away from home and out of state to take this job because I needed experience. This was the job where I would learn what I needed to learn in order to move up in my field! I was demoted because I wasn't ready for my position, and instead of focusing on the negative, I had to realize that the demotion was good for me. It was a blessing. I needed to learn at a slower pace. Never forget that every move you make has a purpose. Always move with intention, and when something is out of your control, move with gratitude and faith.

You're where you are for a reason, and if you learn from a "failure," it's not actually a failure, it's a step. Oprah has even been demoted! She said, "Getting demoted is an opportunity for something else to show up. Getting fired, it puts you in the next best place." Her demotion from a news anchor position led to her talk show, and the rest is history. Her story served as inspiration for me as I navigated the news industry for the first time.

Instead of asking, "Why me?" when you're demoted or fired, just say, "Thank you," and be prepared to elevate. Please remember my story when something in work or life doesn't go how you expected or your way. My mom always tells me to turn an anchor into a missile... I'm unstoppable, and so are you!

RELATED RESOURCE
National Career Development Association
ncda.org

Expressing Yourself

Solution – She Rocked My World

Jada Payne

Once my mom came home, things were different, yet oddly familiar. Having her back made me very happy. I began going to counseling, which I had done eight times in my life before. Through this, I started to understand and come to terms with what had happened. However, when I needed to cope with my emotions, I found solace in one thing — food. People around me encouraged me to eat more and more frequently, and I fell into the habit of using food as my coping mechanism. Most of the time, I ate not because I was hungry, but as a way to deal with my feelings. It took me a long time to realize that my eating had become a serious problem, and the pounds started piling on faster than I could imagine. I lacked someone I could confide in about my problems, and food became my support.

Thankfully, I eventually sought better help from professionals and trusted individuals who guided me back to a healthier path. In the aftermath of the incident, I learned a lot about acceptance. I had to accept that I couldn't change what had happened, but I could continue to grow and thrive. Acceptance became the key to getting my life back on track. Understanding that it wasn't my fault allowed me to bounce back stronger than ever before.

Another important lesson I learned was that others had been through similar experiences. It's okay to talk to someone and seek assistance and answers. You are not alone, and there will always be someone willing to help you.

Bottling up your thoughts and emotions is harmful, and it took me a long time to grasp this truth. Speaking up and ensuring that you are heard and understood is crucial. Feeling alone and misunderstood is normal, but trust me, many others have gone through similar struggles and can offer invaluable support in coping with your emotions. After going through something so stressful, seeking help is your right. Don't hesitate to reach out to a counselor or someone you trust. No one should ever have to suffer in silence about how they feel. Many people have faced challenges far beyond what I could ever know, and talking to survivors and strong individuals can be incredibly helpful.

RELATED RESOURCE
Rainbows
rainbows.org

Trusting His Word

Solution – Why, Oh Why, My Baby Sister?

Saira Whitfield

How did I get through? How do I get through? I felt guilt, anger, frustration, sadness, and pain. I told myself, "I should've stayed home." I tried to blame God; I was so upset. I told myself I wouldn't go to church. I know who God is, and I've been going to my church since I was a baby. That's all I know. I got baptized and filled with the Holy Ghost in Jesus' name, and I thought to blame God and get upset at Him.

Thank God He gave me mercy, but I didn't understand why. "Lord, why would you take away my sister? WHY?" I didn't think it was fair; she didn't have to go — she was only one year old. My pastor always said, "God does things for a reason." It didn't ring true until God reminded me of the Sunday school lesson I had had before this happened.

My sister was taken to be with God. Her funeral was a way of bringing people together — people we didn't know, people we

hadn't seen in a long time, and people who my family didn't necessarily get along with — all came to my baby sister's funeral. It was a time of healing for everyone. It's crazy how God works to reach people. So, how did I get through this? I didn't get through it, at least not by myself. I had God, and He was with me through that whole process of frustration and pain. I thank God He kept my parents and my whole family together. If it weren't for God, our whole family would've been torn apart. Usually, one would leave after a tragedy like this. There would have been no coming back from that. But God, I can't give the credit to anybody but God.

I had to pray, and constantly pray for Him to lift me out of those deep feelings. He pulled me through it. He let me go there, let me get how I felt out, and then He reminded me why He does what He does. It took me a minute to realize that God does all of what He does for a reason. And that my little sister is in a better place away

from all the pain and things of this world. She's protected.

Going through a traumatic experience is hard; things happen, and you can't go through them on your own. With God, you can get through it all. If it weren't for God, I wouldn't be telling others about it. Lord knows I wouldn't even be alive. The mindset and the emotions took me in so many different directions. He kept me in his hands even when I doubted him, even when I said "This is your fault." And because He is my father and my best friend, He allowed me to get it off my chest because He knew the tough time I was going through. Once I was done complaining, crying, and throwing a tantrum, He reminded me of why He does things, and it's never out of hate or revenge.

Going through that time, I had to pray, not only for myself but for my family. We all had to stay strong for each other and pray. When times are tough, pray for yourself and for your family. Pray that

God keeps you, that He keeps your mindset right, that you don't drift away, that He keeps you right where you are.

Prayer changes things, and you can't lose faith through this because you cannot go through a tragedy without a helping hand. And although we have family there with us, God is the ONLY one that will know exactly what you're going through and teach you how to cope. God can be your therapist, that shoulder to cry on, your strength, and your healing.

"Casting all your care upon Him; for He careth for you."
1 Peter 5:7 KJV.

RELATED RESOURCE
Faithful Central Bible Church Youth Ministry
faithfulcentral.com/children-youth

Knowing My Purpose

Solution – A Desire for More

Jasmine Johnson

The first step I took towards building myself up was when I enrolled in cosmetology school and later got my license. Second, I got involved in community college and started working on my general education. When I obtained my cosmetology license, it opened several doors for me. I met so many different types of people and started to gain more confidence as they began to see my beauty on the inside.

Through the connections that I made, I was able to kick-start my career. I have come a long way, but I'm here to say that you never know what's going to happen in life. Just because you're going through tough times now doesn't mean it will always be that way.

RELATED RESOURCE
Los Angeles Urban League
laul.org

Haymali Owens

Since my mother's passing, my brother, sister and I are closer than ever. Before my mom died, my sister and I were not on speaking terms because she never made time for me. She never called me and always broke her promises about coming to see me — just like my mom would do. I didn't know that my mom had another child until Cyncire was one year old. I was never able to see him or spend time with him because no one would communicate on how to set that up. Now everybody always asks me how I am coping with this. I tell them that everything is going to be all right and that there's nothing to worry about anymore because she is in a better place. I tell them that she is watching over me, and that everything gets better with time.

My mother's death taught me to forgive and not hold grudges, and not lose contact with close loved ones. Most of all appreciate your loved ones and never take them for granted. Be thankful for what you have in front of you and for you. Be grateful for what you have. In conclusion, to celebrate my mom, my siblings divided her ashes into portions and put them into a vial necklace. We all wear it with her ashes inside because we wanted her close to our hearts, and what better way than to do that than to put it into a locket? My new saying that I live by now is "Appreciate your loved ones while they are here with you because they can be gone the very next day."

RELATED RESOURCE
What's Your Grief?
whatsyourgrief.com

Seeing the Beauty Within

Solution — Through Thick & Thin

Anonymous

Throughout this two-and-a-half-year journey, I spent a lot of time all over the UCLA medical campus seeing different specialists, and I have always been greeted with a smile. I always try to maintain a positive attitude through thick and thin. There have been days when I thought the world was ending, but thinking with that attitude just makes everything and everyone seem horrible. Some days, I felt like my health was the reason my life was created, as if it were my "punishment" for something I did in the past.

Over time, I've learned that we are all on Earth for a purpose, and I believe my purpose is to teach others the beauty within themselves. If you really dig down, you can find the good in yourself to show others. Maintaining a positive attitude towards things, I was able to find my group of friends who love me for who I am and care for my well-being. Being surrounded by the right friends and having the right mentality is key. Additionally, I found some adults in my life whom I know I can go talk to. I am still dealing with this healing situation, but I'm happy to say that the Lord keeps blessing me to see the sun the next day. On a good note, just remember that there is always someone out there who loves you.

RELATED RESOURCE
UCLA Simms/Mann Center
simmsmanncenter.ucla.edu

Building Confidence

Solution – Is Beauty Only Skin Deep?

Shelbie Wayne

Now that I'm a senior in college and looking back, I am very grateful for the experiences I had growing up. Stepping into college, I learned that what I experienced in my youth does not change in adulthood. But what does change is your reaction and how someone handles certain situations.

I learned to not put so much pressure on myself to be someone I am not because I will just keep on disappointing myself.

I also learned that the truer to yourself you are, the more blessings and fruitful relationships come your way. Never try to please someone else before pleasing yourself. At the end of the day, you must live with YOU for the rest of your life so ask this: Is it better to have peace within yourself or with the world? Self-love is a never-ending journey, but there is beauty in every aspect of that journey. Remind yourself to be more compassionate and understanding, because fighting with yourself will only make it harder.

Decide who you want to be and nourish that person. The world's opinion is just an opinion and has no hold on your journey. I wish my younger self understood this more. But I am glad that I am learning and understanding that now.

RELATED RESOURCE
Resource
website

Depending on God

Solution – Really Felt Like an Outcast

Jazzmin Bates

Though I loved my siblings and was happy for them, a part of me was jealous and envious. I had a void that I felt would never be filled and complete. I didn't have the greatest relationship with my stepfather, and my biological father was in and out of my life. So, I began to look for love in guys. Having boyfriends who helped fill my void temporarily, but never satisfying what I needed. That's when I drew closer to the Lord. I remember one day when I was about fourteen years old. I bawled like a baby and cried on my bed. I prayed and sobbed about wanting a deeper love, wanting to feel whole and complete, and not be the black sheep. I'll never forget the words of the Lord, He said, "You are my daughter, and I am your father." I remember falling on my face and for the first time I felt embraced in the arms of my Heavenly Father. A love that I'd never felt. Daily, whether that be walking, in my room, or in the bathroom, I began to build a relationship with the Lord. Finding myself talking aloud as if He were there in the flesh. There were nights we laughed and nights I cried, but I always felt His comfort and unconditional love.

I also began journaling. I started writing any feelings, thoughts, desires and prayers down. Some letters and prayers I wrote were prayers of forgiveness. Forgiving my parents and releasing the anger I felt towards them for my brokenness. The Lord showed me through His word that what was meant to break me and wound me, the Lord will turn it around for my good.

Though I was born out of wedlock, raised in a blended family, had daddy issues, boy issues, teen issues, love issues, I would now be able to look back and say, "I have overcome." Today I'm able to share my testimony and help encourage others to overcome their trials and change the next generation. Now I am twenty-nine years old, and the Lord has answered one of my biggest prayers. That "One day I wanted to be married and have children." I do believe we have the power to leave the negative and take the positive and change the negative things that affected you to carry and pass down the positive to the next generation.

As we continue to gain wisdom, knowledge, revelation and understanding daily to make those changes. I am blessed to have a husband who's an amazing husband and father to our children, and seeing the love and joy he gives to our children has brought joy to my soul knowing my prayers have been fulfilled.

Many children are raised in broken homes and blended families. Though no household is perfect, we can learn from our past and help to make a better future. I encourage everyone to have hope and faith and know that you have the power to overcome your trials and tribulations, rather than your problems overcoming YOU.

RELATED RESOURCE
Open Paths Counseling Center
openpaths.org

Believing I'm Worthy

Solution – Misconceptions & Perceptions About My Skin Tone

Trinity Fuller

By the end of my senior year, I began to self-reflect and realized all my fears and worries really were irrational for so many years. I put care and love into all that I cared about, and no matter what other people may think of me, I was good enough for whatever came my way. Just because I looked different didn't mean that I was an awful person. I graduated as a semi-confident seventeen-year-old and felt much more confident for college.

Now that I'm older and in college, I've learned that although I am different, I'm still beautiful and talented and valued in society. There are so many special parts of myself and my community that I could ever try to hide because they make me unique. The societal preferences and discrimination that has occurred can make it easy for any Black girl to lose hope in themself, but as I am growing, I am learning to accept the person that I am. There is beauty in every person, but at a certain point in many girls' lives, the innocence and love dissipate due to society's standards.

I enter places with a different kind of confidence that I didn't have growing up and it's good feeling confident in a new space. I think it all started by telling myself that I was worthy. Not letting negativity get into my head and affect the things I cared about. The respect I gave to myself, and letting myself be kinder, then made me think I was beautiful on the outside as well.

I think the experiences I had as a child did make me much stronger as well, because I learned to love myself completely. I hope over the next coming years I love all parts of me wholly. It feels great to completely love myself after so many years of discomfort in my skin. It feels great to be in such a positive headspace once and for all.

RELATED RESOURCE
Psychology Help
psychologyhelp.com

Connecting

Rocky Avalos

Though I still have cycles of all my issues, they have significantly lessened. At a young age, my aunt took me to a homeopathic doctor, a hybrid of a therapist and psychiatrist who prescribed homeopathic remedies and provided life advice. The two homeopathic doctors I have seen have been life-changing for me. While such doctors may not be for everyone, the takeaway is that there are people, whether professionals or not, who can help you through rough patches in life and support you even when you think you're fine and no longer need help. Please know that there is someone out there who feels similar to you, who can relate to your experiences. And even if there's someone who can't fully relate, they may still be willing to lend a supportive shoulder.

Another important thing! Always keep your interests close to you — pursue them and practice them regularly. Don't underestimate the power of your passions, whether it's music, art, reading, being outdoors, video games, coding, or anything else that ignites your enthusiasm. For me, those public elementary school art classes, the Concepts in a Box film program by La Faye, and the music that inspired my art, film, and music interests were pivotal. Without them, I might have only seen my life as a constant struggle. Looking back at middle school, high school, college, and now, I can recognize all the mental health challenges I faced, but I can also

recall the fun and exciting times with family and friends.

The laughs we shared and the joy I brought out in others remind me that not all the positivity in our lives comes from external sources; it also emanates from within us. We have the power to bring joy to others and uplift situations, and it's important to recognize our ability to spread positivity.

Because we aren't the only ones needing help to get out of a hard place, when others need help, we provide it to them too. We become part of the lives and histories of other people, where we are important and integral to their happiness. To quote the beloved Mister Rogers, "When I was a boy and I would see scary things in the news, my mother would say to me, 'Look for the helpers. You will always find people who are helping.'" Always look for those who are helping you or are capable of helping you, and cherish all the things, loves, interests, and places that have been helping you or others. Help, love, and support are out there, and they are welcoming to you.

RELATED RESOURCE
Los Angeles LGBT Center
lalgbtcenter.org

Inspirational Resources

Podcasts

- Diamond in the RAW Girls Teens 12-18 | Anchor
    - Brooklyn in the Haus (Brookleynn Fenderson)
    - Teen Life (Saira Whitfield)
    - Behind the Singer (Angel Boyd)
    - Netflix (Ryan Kazadi)
    - Jenuine with Jada (Jada Payne)
    - Mayaneko and the World of Gaming (Chole Howard)
- Therapy for Black Girls | Amazon Music
- The Girl Defined Show | Amazon Music
- Dear Teen Girls | Apple Music
- Black Girls Heal | Apple Music
- Brown Love | Spotify
- Teenage Therapy| Spotify
- Hardcore Self-Help | Spotify
- She Persisted | Spotify
- On Our Minds | Spotify

Uplifting Music

- Teen Girl Talk | Apple Music
- This is Normal | Apple Music
- Koryn Hawthorne: All Songs | Spotify

Books

- *I Am Enough*
- *I Choose to Try Again*
- *Skin Like Mine*
- *The Me I Choose to Be*
- *Making Mistakes Are How I Learn*
- *Be Unapologetically You*
- *The Lonely Girl in the Universe*
- *Raw Emotions of a Black Girl*
- *Life Skills: A Teens Girls Guide to Beating Worry and Anxiety*
- *Empowered Black Girl: Joyful Affirmations and Words of Resilience*
- *The Self-Love*
- *Jump Start Confidence*
- *Year of Positive Thinking for Teens*
- *Mindfulness for Teens in 10 minutes*
- *Highly Effective Teens*
- *The Body Image Book for Girls*
- *Jump Start Confidence*
- *Words of Wisdom for Teens*
- *5 Simple Steps of Managing Your Moods*
- *Hey Brown Girl*

My Future Resolution

My Future Resolution

My Future Resolution

My Future Resolution

My Future Resolution

411 On Mental Health

Everybody experiences mental health to some degree. It is simply a state of well-being in which a person can cope with the various stresses of life to reach their full potential. This state encompasses both emotional and physical health, as well as a person's ability to interact well with others, as meaningful relationships are affected by our state of mind.

Mental health can significantly impact day-to-day activities, making it an essential part of overall health. It is influenced by a combination of biological and environmental factors, including genetics, lifestyle, and stress levels. Mental health affects individuals of all ages, genders, and backgrounds, and its severity can vary from mild to severe. For instance, in one of our stories, a young woman's mental health journey led her from experiencing mild depression to developing schizophrenia, highlighting how serious mental health issues can be.

The CDC emphasizes that when a teen is struggling with a mental health condition, it can profoundly impact all aspects of their lives. Academic performance may decline, difficulties with social relationships may persist, and negative changes in various behaviors and habits may occur, causing stress within the family dynamic. Seeking professional treatment for adolescents experiencing mood disorders or psychiatric distress is imperative to restore healthy functioning.

Depression is especially pervasive among many high school and college students, influenced by social aspects such as lifestyles, grades, exclusion in groups, bullying, family, socioeconomic status, and traumas such as sexual violence. According to the CDC, in 2021, 2 in 5 of all high school students experienced persistent feelings of sadness and hopelessness that affected their daily life. Over 50% of young women reported feeling this way that year, and rates of poor mental health continue to increase. Disturbingly, 30% of females teens seriously considered attempting suicide and 1 in 4 made a plan in the past year. When considering students who identify as LGBQ+, the rates of depression and suicide are even higher.[1]

It is crucial to address solutions for depression and mental health issues promptly. Mental health is vital for everyone, and seeking help is essential if you are feeling overwhelmed or struggling with any mental health challenges. Remember, reaching out for support is a sign of strength, and professional assistance can make a significant difference in improving one's well-being.

If you are having suicidal thoughts, you can call or text 988 for 24/7 free and confidential support. Learn more at 988lifeline.org.

---

1 All statistics from the CDC's 2011-2021 "Youth Risk Behavior Survey Data Summary & Trends Report" available at https://www.cdc.gov/healthyyouth/mental-health/index.htm

About Depression

Depression is a mood disorder that affects around 280 million people across the globe.[1] In the U.S., 5 million people ages 12–17 suffer from depression.[2] This complex condition has mental and physical symptoms that interfere with someone's ability to function day-to-day. Recognizing symptoms of depression can help in understanding the situation and seeking help.

Below are some common signs of depression.[3] If you are noticing any of these symptoms for at least two weeks or think you may be depressed, talk with a parent, teacher, school counselor, friend or anyone you trust who can help you get the support you need. You can also call SAMHSA's National Helpline at 800-662-HELP (4357).

PHYSICAL	EMOTIONAL
• disrupted or too much sleep	• deep sadness
• change in eating habits	• easily irritated
• loss or gain in weight	• worrisome or anxious
• persistent headaches or pain	• hopeless about future
RELATIONAL	**FUNCTIONAL**
• withdrawn from activities	• difficulty concentrating
• lost interest in relationships	• lack of motivation
• increased conflict	• unhealthy habits
• feelings of emptiness	• suicidal thoughts

1 https://vizhub.healthdata.org/gbd-results/
2 https://www.nimh.nih.gov/health/statistics/major-depression
3 See QR codes to the right

There are nine types of depression:[1]

- Major Depression — Can be a single episode of depression lasting weeks or months or experienced throughout life
- Persistent Depression — Two or more years of depression
- Bipolar Disorder — Mood alternates between depressive episode and mania or hypomania that lasts at least seven days
- Depressive Psychosis — Can involve hallucinations and delusions
- Perinatal Depression — During pregnancy or within four weeks of giving birth
- Premenstrual Dyshphoric Disorder — Timing related to hormonal changes; symptoms more severe and disruptive than PMS
- Seasonal Depression — Related to season changes, usually winter
- Situational Depression — Brought on by specific event or circumstance; feelings and symptoms interfere with functioning
- Atypical Depression — Depressive episodes that go away for a period when a positive event or situation happens

LEARN MORE ABOUT SYMPTOMS & TREATMENTS:

SAMHSA | World Health Organization | Nemours TeensHealth | Mayo Clinic

---

1 https://www.healthline.com/health/types-of-depression

Acknowledgments

I would first of all like to thank God, along with those responsible for my life and creative vision — my heavenly Father and Mother Bill and Viola Baker. You have been an inspiration and prepared me for this journey called life.

Indeed, it is with a profound sense of gratitude that I acknowledge the abundant blessings and visionary insights that have brought this inspirational book to fruition. Each blessing, a radiant beam of light illuminating the path forward, and each vision, a tapestry of aspirations woven with threads of hope and determination, have converged to manifest this literary masterpiece into existence.

Without the bountiful blessings bestowed upon me and the clarity of vision that guided my steps, this transformative work would remain but a distant dream, confined to the recesses of imagination. It is through the benevolent grace of providence and the unwavering clarity of purpose that this book now graces the shelves, ready to inspire hearts and minds with its profound message of resilience and triumph.

Moreover, without the myriad blessings bestowed upon me and the clarity of vision that has guided my path, this inspirational book would never have seen the light of day.

As I reflect upon the journey that has led me to this moment, I am humbled by the realization that every blessing, every vision, has played an integral role in shaping the narrative of this book. Indeed, it is a testament to the power of divine intervention and human endeavor, converging in harmony to bring forth a literary testament that will endure the test of time.

A profound and heartfelt thank you resonates deeply within me as I reflect on the journey I've undertaken. To all those who've walked alongside me: Your steadfast presence, encouraging words,

friendship, love, and alliance have illuminated my path, propelled me forward, and nurtured my growth. Among the constellation of guiding lights, I extend my deepest gratitude to individuals like Adai Lamar (KJLH), Darrell Brown, Arna Fulcher, Regina Davis, Novel Harris, Katherine Cooper, Alisha Bonner, Carrie Bernans, Radshida Tinkshell, Ceret Daramola, Elaine Theus, Karen Brown, Carrie Henley, Harriett Mitchell, Deandra Duncan, Lori A. Alston, Yinka Adeboyeku, Toya Mack-Burton, Charlie Lowe, Dani Burton, Kiara Lainer, Dajai Davis, Jannie McKinney, Maleena Lawerence, Patricia Lee-Stolberg, Kenya Ware, Mixed Chicks, Wendi Levy and Kim Etheredge, plus countless others and my esteemed Sorority Sisters of Delta Sigma Theta Sorority Inc. I hold each of you in the highest esteem.

Heartfelt and enduring thanks to my heavenly Sisterfriend, Donna Lambert Dunbar, for her unwavering encouragement, listening ear, and steadfast support. You will be eternally remembered and forever remain in my heart.

Special appreciation is reserved for Roqui Theus, my goddaughter, whose radiant spirit and Emmy Award-winning talents have been a source of constant inspiration. Roqui, your kindness, encouragement, and unwavering support have infused my journey with joy and purpose.

In this moment of reflection, I am compelled to extend heartfelt recognition to the remarkable young women whose captivating stories grace the pages of this book. Your presence within these narratives has imbued this journey with depth, authenticity, and profound resonance.

Each of you have brought a unique perspective and a wealth of experiences, enriching the tapestry of this collective narrative in ways beyond measure. I am deeply touched by your willingness to

open your hearts and minds, and I hold each of you in the highest esteem. Your voices echo with authenticity and power, illuminating the path for others to follow.

Furthermore, I extend my gratitude to Michelle King and the Board of Directors, along with the volunteers, of Diamond in the RAW nonprofit 501c3. Thank you also to the teenage girls who have been part of the program. Your presence and participation have added immeasurable depth to this journey of discovery. Through your interactions and shared experiences, you have illuminated the profound truth that life is not merely a destination, but a transformative journey guided by purpose and meaning.

About La Faye Baker

La Faye Baker, a vibrant product of the inner city and a former probation officer, passionately champions the cause of teen girls, fervently dedicated to bolstering their self-esteem and nurturing their confidence to pave the way for triumphant success.

With an unwavering resolve, she endeavors to stem the tide of despair, combat human trafficking, and illuminate the vital importance of seeking counseling for those grappling with inner turmoil. Her tireless efforts are infused with a profound commitment to reshaping communities, eradicating the specter of suicide, and fostering a future where hope reigns supreme.

Renowned as the inspiring founder of the Diamond in the RAW 501c3 nonprofit organization, a beacon of hope illuminating the paths of foster care and at-risk teen girls through the transformative power of the arts, La Faye epitomizes resilience and compassion.

Her indomitable spirit has catalyzed profound change in the lives of countless young women, weaving narratives of triumph and resilience amidst adversity. Within the pages of her inspiring book, *You're Not Listening to... What I Have to Say*, tales abound of teens who have emerged as resilient victors, propelled by the programs she has spearheaded, surmounting the trials of adolescence with courage and grace. A trailblazer unafraid to challenge the status quo, La Faye stands as a testament to the enduring impact of visionary leadership and unwavering dedication to the greater good.

Furthermore she stands as the visionary architect behind the prestigious Action Icon Stuntwomen's Awards, a groundbreaking

platform dedicated to shining a spotlight on the unsung heroes and heroines of the stunt community within action-oriented films and television. With unparalleled foresight and unwavering dedication, she has carved out a space to honor the fearless individuals who risk life and limb to bring heart-stopping action sequences to life on the silver screen. Through her leadership, she has transformed the landscape of recognition within the industry, ensuring that the remarkable contributions of stuntwomen are celebrated and revered for generations to come.

La Faye's illustrious career spans over two decades in the dynamic realm of the entertainment industry, where she has fearlessly dazzled audiences as a distinguished professional stuntwoman. Her unparalleled expertise has garnered acclaim and accolades from City Officials and community-based organizations, acknowledging her profound impact on the community. Featured prominently in a myriad of articles and television specials, she has captivated audiences with her remarkable journey as a trailblazing stunt performer, inspiring countless aspiring talents along the way.

Firmly rooted in her belief that every life journey is a profound lesson waiting to be embraced, she espouses the transformative power of the three D's of success: Determination, Dedication, and Discipline. These formidable virtues serve as the bedrock of her unparalleled achievements, infusing her breathtaking stunts with an electrifying blend of skill and tenacity.

A consummate scholar, La Faye possesses a distinguished academic pedigree, boasting a BS from California State University Long Beach. She has further honed her craft through the prestigious Film Entertainment and Digital Media Program at UCLA, acquiring invaluable insights into the ever-evolving landscape of the entertainment industry. Her pursuit of excellence also led her to earn an MBA from the University of Miami, solidifying her prowess as a multifaceted force to be reckoned with in both academia and the entertainment world. Additionally, her affiliations include esteemed organizations such as the Delta Sigma Theta Sorority Inc., LAAAWPPI, WSource, AABLI and SAG-AFTRA.

She emerges as an unparalleled pioneer, not only in the realm of professionalism and commitment within the stunt community but also in her unwavering dedication to service within underserved communities. Her trailblazing spirit and tireless efforts have set a new standard of excellence, inspiring others to follow in her footsteps and make a meaningful impact both on and off the screen.

Solutions
to explore

Turn
the book over

My Current Circumstances

My Current Circumstances

My Current Circumstances

My Current Circumstances